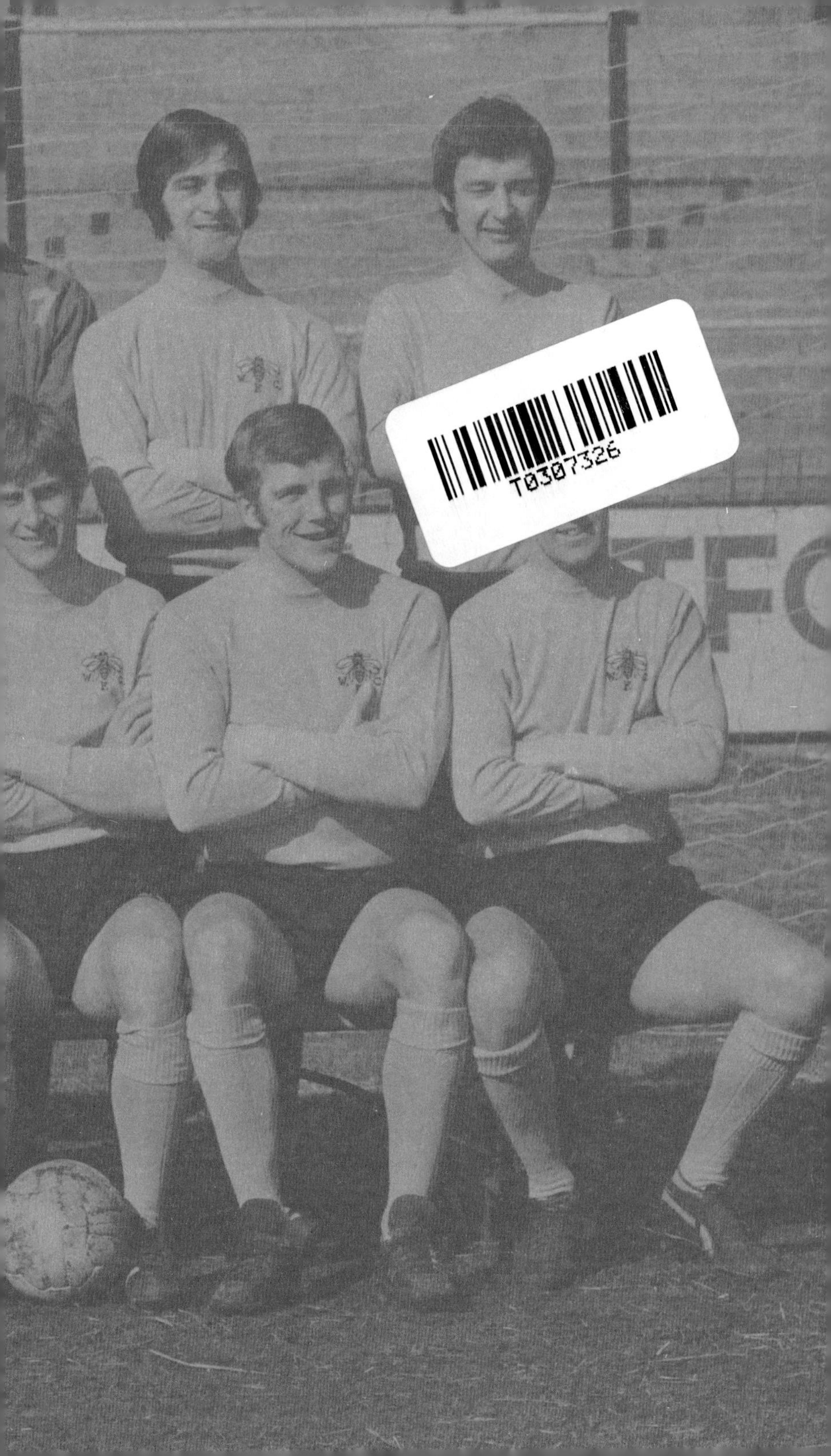

From FATHER *to* SON

From FATHER *to* SON

How Fate and Family
Made Me a Watford Fan

PAUL BISHOP

pitch

First published by Pitch Publishing, 2021

Pitch Publishing
A2 Yeoman Gate
Yeoman Way
Worthing
Sussex
BN13 3QZ
www.pitchpublishing.co.uk
info@pitchpublishing.co.uk

A CIP catalogue record is available for this book
from the British Library.

ISBN 978 1 78531 760 6

Typesetting and origination by Pitch Publishing

Printed and bound in India by Replika Press Pvt. Ltd.

Contents

Acknowledgements

I WOULD like to dedicate this book to my father, Geoff Bishop, who introduced me to the fun and thrills of watching football, and my mother, Joyce, for achieving a one hundred per cent record – one Watford match attended, one win. And what a win!

Eric Idle sang about always looking on the bright side of life, and I know what he means. Putting a book together is a serious business, but I've had such fun writing and researching this book whilst the rest of the country has been in meltdown coping with Covid-19. Big thanks to all my friends, family and fellow fans for helping me put this book together and guiding me on my trip down memory lane. People like Luther Blissett, and Oliver Phillip, who responded rapidly and courteously to my queries and questions, even when he was holidaying in France! Thanks also to Jon Berry, Geoff Watts and Peter Lingham for their written contributions on those marvellous footballing days with St Albans Wanderers, and also Matthew Smith, Jim Campbell and Paul and Roger Baker for reading the proofs. Alun Lewis deserves a mention for giving me the *Historic Newspapers – Watford* scrapbook as a birthday present a few years back. And not forgetting my brother, Laurie, an early companion, home and away.

The *Old Watford* website proved to be quite a find; so useful for facts, figures and features. *The BBC Archive* and *At Home with Colin Murray* were amusing and informative sources in helping me piece together the profiles of Luther Blissett and John Barnes. Similarly, Kevin Affleck's interview with Tom Walley on *Watford Legends* was a fascinating insight on how Tom managed and nurtured young players so successfully.

Enjoy the Game, Lionel Birnie's excellent account of the Graham Taylor/Elton John era, and Matt Rowson's *Watford FC On This Day* were both helpful books, as were *Billy Wright: A Hero for All Seasons, Puskas on Puskas,* Arthur Hopcraft's *The Football Man,* Jack Rosenthal's *By Jack Rosenthal – An Autobiography in Six Acts* and *A Man For All Seasons: Brian Owen's Six-Decade Football Odyssey.* David McVay's *Steak Diana Ross* is a witty account of his time playing for Notts County during the 1970s. His brief but memorable descriptions of a chain-smoking Ian Bolton walking around under a perpetual cloud of cigarette smoke have stayed with me since reading the book several years ago.

I must give heartfelt thanks to my lovely (and patient) wife, Begoña, and also Elia and Harry for allowing me to use the kitchen table as a work base over the spring and summer months of 2020.

Finally, not forgetting the friendly and helpful people at Pitch – another great team!

Paul Bishop
SEPTEMBER 2020

Foreword
by Luther Blissett

'GET YOURSELF a proper trade and work hard' … words my father said when I told him that I had been offered a contract to become a professional footballer. He was a carpenter by trade so had been creating things his whole life and that's the kind of future he saw for his son, having come to England from Jamaica to build a solid life for us. He knew hard work was the way to have a decent life.

I had already received confirmation of an apprenticeship to train as a motor technician at a local garage and he simply could not see there was a choice to be made. I had a passion for cars, loved the technology behind them and the challenge of getting a machine to work. But then I had started to play football and discover the thrill of scoring goals, albeit in the streets and the local park. Creating those winning scores even with my friends had a magic all of its own and a possibility for a life a boy could only dream of.

My mother's words when I told her what dad thought were more or less the same, but she added something. 'Follow your dream, Luther. Work hard, listen and try to do the things asked of you to the very best of your ability, then you will achieve whatever you want.'

Those words were then repeated by the man who throughout my career as a footballer at Watford FC became very much my second father, Graham Taylor OBE. Football brought us together and forged that special bond, as only football can through many generations of fathers to sons.

Introduction

> What is a club in any case? Not the buildings or directors or the people who are paid to represent it. It's not the television contracts, get-out clauses, marketing departments or executive boxes.
>
> It's the noise, the passion, the feeling of belonging, the pride in your city. It's a small boy clambering up stadium steps for the first time, gripping his father's hand, gawping at that hallowed stretch of turf beneath him and, without being able to do a thing about it, falling in love – **Sir Bobby Robson**

PEOPLE OF a certain age remember Friday, 22 November 1963 as the day when President John Kennedy was assassinated in Dallas and Aldous Huxley died in Los Angeles. But for Watford fans, that date will always be known as the day Duncan Welbourne signed professional forms for the club.

However, Friday, 23 March 1962 was the day that changed my life and it was all Jimmy Hill's fault. Hill was the manager of Coventry City, the visitors at Vicarage Road on that fateful day. My dad wanted to pay tribute to the former chairman of the Professional Footballers' Association. A year earlier Hill had been instrumental in ending the Football League's maximum wage of £20 a week. Almost immediately, Hill's former Fulham team-mate Johnny Haynes became the game's first £100-a-week player. Dad didn't want to visit the game alone so he took his youngest son – me. Although I was too small to see any of the game, I was hooked.

And so began a lifetime of devotion, and also a little misery mixed with fear. And it wasn't just fear of defeat. Watching football in the late 1960s and early 1970s was often a risky and violent business, both on and off the pitch. Most sides had at least one hardman in defence; Chelsea had Ron 'Chopper' Harris, Manchester United had Nobby Stiles, Liverpool Tommy Smith and Leeds had an assortment of assassins including Billy Bremner, Norman Hunter and Johnny Giles. It might have been 'the beautiful game' in Pelé's eyes, but for a young English fan you had to watch out for fists, coins and bovver boots. Yes, this is the story of trips to Walsall, Exeter, Mansfield, Shrewsbury, Swansea, Luton, Gillingham and Bury in those early Graham Taylor 'family club' days. It takes a look back at some of the memorable games and some of the lesser-known players who were to become folk heroes on the terraces of Vicarage Road. Players like Tom Walley, Terry Garbett and Dennis Booth, as well as more recognised stars like John Barnes, Luther Blissett, Ross Jenkins and Tony Coton.

August 2020

Since I began writing this book, a number of the players mentioned within its pages have sadly passed away. These include Jack Charlton and Alan Garner. By all accounts, Jack Charlton was as genuine a person as you could wish to meet.

He seemed to truly enjoy the good and simple things in life, whether that was trout fishing in Ireland or a few quiet drinks after the game. Writer and broadcaster Danny Baker has a particular tale to tell: 'Possibly my favourite football story of all is how the morning after the World Cup Final, Jack Charlton woke up on the living room floor of a couple from Dagenham he had no recollection of meeting. His winner's medal was still in his pocket.'

Whereas Jack's eyes always twinkled, younger brother Bobby had a sadder countenance, possibly caused by the trauma he experienced during and immediately after the Munich air crash in 1958. Jack tells the tale of when he learnt of his first England cap after the FA Cup semi-final against Manchester United in 1965: 'We won 1-0 and went back to the dressing room where we found lots of booze – whisky and beer and everything. I had a bottle of beer and sat down when Don Revie came in and said he wanted a word with me now as he didn't want to tell me before because he might have put me off my game. He said I'd been selected to play against Scotland at Wembley in May and I said "Me?" He said yes and that all the lads knew and they all congratulated me. So I thought I've got to tell our kid. So I went into their dressing room and went across to him and said: "Hey kidda, you'll never believe this but I've been selected to play for England with you against the Scots." And he sat there looking a bit depressed and said: "I'm pleased for you." I was completely out of order. I mean, you don't go into the dressing room of the team you've just beaten in a cup semi-final. Even Denis [Law] didn't like me for doing that.'

Like Jack Charlton, Alan Garner was a dependable defender, which in the third and fourth tier of English football during the mid-70s was exactly what you needed. When he was joined by Ian Bolton in 1977, they made the perfect partnership; as a supporter you felt reassured when those two were on the team sheet …

After signing from local rivals Luton in 1975, Garner was an ever-present for a second consecutive season when Watford won the Fourth Division championship in 1977/78, earning the Player of the Season title.

A powerful defender with a memorable long throw, Garner then missed only four games when another promotion was secured the following season. He made a total of 232 appearances with 16 goals across six seasons of sterling service to the club. 'Winning at Manchester United and claiming the Fourth Division championship were the highlights,' Alan said.

CHAPTER 1
Jimmy, Johnny and George

YES, I blame Jimmy Hill. In between playing inside-right for Brentford and Fulham and fronting several successful football shows on TV, Hill, in his dual role as manager of Coventry City and chairman of the Professional Footballers' Association, successfully abolished the Football League's maximum wage in 1961. A keen trade union leader, Hill brought to an end the miserly £20 weekly pay packet, resulting in his former Fulham colleague Johnny Haynes becoming the first £100-a-week player. Haynes and Hill were not alone in feeling pleased about all this; some 30 miles north of Craven Cottage, in leafy Hertfordshire, my father, Geoff, was equally ecstatic …

During the latter period of Hill's career – when he was a regular presenter and pundit on both ITV and BBC – he was often perceived as a figure of fun by public and media alike. Hill was never shy and would often play up to the media, displaying his long chin and pipe in a comical fashion in many press photos. He also once memorably replaced an injured linesman and ran enthusiastically up and down the line in a televised match. However, it must be acknowledged that Hill was a clever and forward-thinking operator. His many innovations as manager at Coventry revolutionised the club as well as the game in general. For instance, he immediately nicknamed the club The Sky Blue Revolution, changed the kit to light blue and co-wrote the club's 'Sky Blue Song'. He also introduced the first magazine-style club programme and encouraged fans to get to the brand-new stadium early to enjoy the pre-match entertainment.

A year or so after Hill's victory, I remember Dad mentioning the name George Eastham a few times. I presumed it was because Eastham was rated as a skilful inside-forward, similar to Haynes. But there was another reason. Eastham, who was born in Blackpool in 1936, joined Newcastle United some 20 years later. During his time there he fell out with the club, claiming the house the club had supplied him with was uninhabitable. He also had issues with the secondary job that the club had arranged for him and their attempts to stop him playing for the England U23 team. With his contract due to expire soon, in 1959, Eastham refused to sign a new one and requested a transfer. However, Newcastle refused to let Eastham go.

Unable to leave, Eastham went on strike at the end of the 1959/60 season, moving south to work as a salesman. Finally, in October 1960 Newcastle relented and sold Eastham to Arsenal for £47,500. However, Eastham considered the point worth fighting for and, backed by the PFA – who provided £15,000 to pay for Eastham's legal fees – he took the club to the High Court in 1963.

In the case, *Eastham versus Newcastle,* Eastham argued that it was an unfair restraint of trade and that Newcastle owed him £400 in unpaid wages and £650 in unpaid bonuses. The judge ruled partly in Eastham's favour, stating that the retain-and-transfer system was unreasonable, although he ruled that, as Eastham had refused to play for Newcastle, any payment of wages for the disputed period was at Newcastle's discretion. Although Eastham did not gain personally, he succeeded in reforming the British transfer market. The 'retain' element of retain-and-transfer was greatly reduced, providing fairer terms for players looking to re-sign for their clubs, and setting up a transfer tribunal for disputes.

Dad was a staunch socialist whose regular reading material included *Tribune, Private Eye* and *ERT* (Electrical Retail Trader). Hill and Eastham quickly became heroes of my father, ranking just below a non-footballer – Nye Bevan, Labour MP and founder of the NHS. Coincidentally, Bevan had been co-editor of *Tribune* between 1941 and 1945. At this time my father had other more pressing priorities, training to drive a tank and being posted to north Africa before travelling to Arnhem, Holland to fight the good and futile fight there.

He didn't do things by halves though and, after surviving Arnhem by the skin of his false teeth, having somehow escaped his shell-blasted tank on three separate occasions, he returned home to find a wife, raise a family and get a job, not necessarily in that order.

He accomplished all three and, a year after Hill's great wages triumph, Coventry City visited Watford, which was the nearest league club to our Bricket Wood home. And so on Friday, 23 March 1962, Dad decided to pay his respects to Jimmy in person and arranged a short trip to Vicarage Road to watch the game. He didn't go alone though, he took me along too.

I was going to watch a real football match for the first time and, even at that tender age, I had the feeling that this was going to be an exciting and important day. Although I recall nothing of the actual game, I remember that I stood alongside Dad at the Vicarage Road end. It was no surprise that details of the game are a blur as I was far too short to see anything more than a few fleeting images as I was surrounded by, what seemed like, several hundred huge football-loving giants towering above me.

Bizarrely, the highlight of the day was getting back home in time to hear the result being announced on BBC Radio. By the time my mum had made us a nice cup of tea the result had been solemnly announced. I couldn't believe I had been at the same game when the following words crackled across the airwaves: 'Watford 0, Coventry City 1', especially as it was news to me that my team had lost!

But the result didn't seem to matter that much. The important thing was that Dad had inadvertently cast the soccer spell and I had succumbed to its magic. Arthur Hopcraft, author of *The Football Man,* concurs: 'Even now, whenever I arrive at any football ground, or merely pass close to one when it is silent, I experience a unique alerting of the senses. The moment evokes my past as an instantaneous emotional rapport which is more certain, more secret, than memory.'

I would become a Watford supporter for better or worse, but not immediately. For the next few years I switched my allegiance to Manchester United. This was mainly because the following season I watched my first FA Cup Final on TV. It featured United versus the favourites Leicester City. United, who had struggled in the league that season, triumphed 3-1 with Denis Law scoring a memorable opener past Gordon

Banks. Law immediately became my boyhood hero and not even the emergence of the teenage Beatle-lookalike George Best a few months later could usurp him. I was not alone though. A whole generation of young football fans loved Law and United in equal measure. Why?

I believe the main reason was that the tragedy of the 1958 Munich air disaster was still fresh in the minds of football fans across the globe, and in May 1963 Law was United's newcomer, having arrived for a record fee from a glamorous Italian club – Torino. He was the future, a mercurial Scottish showman, a sportsman born at the right time and in the right place. He was a predator with pace, wit and attitude. Great in the air, he was a constant danger, not only in the penalty area but when picking up the ball from deep and running rapidly at the opposition.

What's more, Law and his team-mates were blessed with a great manager – Matt Busby. Busby must have known he had been similarly blessed with the likes of Law, Best and Bobby Charlton leading their attack and Pat Crerand and Nobby Stiles adding the necessary steel in midfield. Busby was also clever enough to realise that he could let the attack loose on the opposition with the simple instruction: 'Just go out and play.'

There's a story about a pre-match team talk given by legendary Liverpool boss Bill Shankly prior to facing United. Legend has it that Shankly went through the opposition's line-up one by one, singling out the shortcomings and weaknesses of United's line-up. He started with goalkeeper Harry Gregg, old; Shay Brennan, slow; Bill Foulkes, can't head the ball; Tony Dunn, one-footed; Pat Crerand, temperamental; Nobby Stiles, dirty; Albert Quixall, dodgy knees; and David Herd, lazy. He stopped and was about to leave, when one of the Liverpool players said: 'What about Law, Best and Charlton boss?' To which Shankly replied: 'Well if you canna' beat a team with only three players!'

Law had many attributes that attracted young footballers and fans alike. For starters he possessed the best bicycle kick in the game, he was spring-heeled and able to beat many taller defenders in the air, he had the best goal celebrations and he had an arrogant swagger about his game. He also became a style icon by playing whilst gripping the cuffs of his long-sleeved football shirt. Not that important, you might think, except that so many players, pros and amateurs copied him. I've lost count of the number of times I've played with, and against, footballers of a certain age who mimic 'The King'. We might not have been able to play like him, but we could try, in some small way, to look like him. I know fellow football-lover Rod Stewart is a fan and I'm sure he copied Law's hairstyle too! Former West Bromwich Albion striker Tony 'Bomber' Brown was also a huge admirer of Law.

I soon realised that Dad was not an avid football fan. I was sure he liked the game though, and he once told me he played in goal at school and that his boyhood hero was Alex James, the playmaking inside-forward of the great Arsenal side of the mid-1930s. He also told me how good Cliff 'Boy' Bastin was and that James and his team-mates did most of their training in the local *Orange Tree* pub in Totteridge. This was typical of his humour and quite possibly true. But he always had a 'soft spot' for Watford and, although I realised regular trips to watch Watford with Dad wouldn't happen, he always remained interested in the club's fortunes. On my return from a game he would always enquire whether there had been a good attendance and what sort of a game it had been. In time this was abbreviated to one short, swift and simple sentence: 'Many there, good game?'

Dad was acutely aware that in those days – before sponsorship, TV millions and billionaire investors – gate receipts were the main source of income. In Watford's case it was vital, as chairman Jim Bonser had a reputation for being careful with the cash. Lancashire-born Bonser was chairman from 1958 until 1976 and was a hard-nosed businessman who seemed reluctant to invest in the club.

My Dad preferred tennis in his younger days, and he was quite handy too, winning the men's singles at Mill Hill Tennis Club in 1947. He also won the heart of my mum, Joyce, there. Dad often mentioned that Fred Perry was an inspiration. This was hardly surprising as Perry, brought up as a working-class socialist in Stockport, was very much an exception in the tennis world of the 1930s. According to Dad, Perry's hard-hitting, big-serving aggressive game went against the grain of the old boys' hierarchy within the Lawn Tennis Association (LTA) of which Dan Maskell was a leading light. Maskell was at times not keen on Perry and favoured the gentler, more stylish game of Bunny Austin. Perry was an out-and-out winner and Great Britain had to wait another 60 years for another when Scotsman Andy Murray burst onto the scene.

During a holiday in Devon in the early 60s, Dad took the family to watch the British player, Roger Becker, take on Jaroslav Drobny in an exhibition match at Budleigh Salterton Lawn Tennis Club. Becker was a tenacious player from a working-class background in south London. Jaroslav Drobny was born in Prague, Czechoslovakia, leaving the country in 1949 to travel to Egypt where he attained Egyptian citizenship. He later came to the United Kingdom and became a British citizen. In 1954 he beat Ken Rosewall in the Wimbledon men's singles final and, with a formidable left-handed swinging serve, was a handful, particularly on the clay courts of Europe. He won the Italian singles championship three times and the French twice to prove it. But on grass, Becker must have fancied his chances.

The club was jammed with spectators, many of them elderly ladies used to tea and cucumber sandwiches. Instead they got some salty language from Becker, who had already been upset when Drobny set the tone for the match by arriving on court and looking around with a perplexed look on his face: 'No ball boys for a player of my calibre?' he asked nobody in particular. Becker's mood soon blackened when he got a pasting in the first set, he started effing and blinding at the top of his South Norwood voice. Dad found it all highly amusing and the game and Becker's language was often recounted to his friends and drinking partners. On the rare occasions I play club and friendly tennis, I repeat Drobny's remark about the lack of ball boys. I think Dad would have liked that.

Dad also played the occasional round of golf at Batchwood in nearby St Albans, but it was often a trial. When I once asked him how he had played, he replied: 'One good one, one bad one.' When I was older I often thought that was not a bad average! However, his father was a good player at Finchley Golf Club, just a five-minute walk from his home. My grandfather, Alfred, was a kind, courteous and calm man, less than average height and not a big hitter. Dad told me that Alfred was uncannily accurate off the tee, hardly ever straying from the fairway, and possessed an impressive 'short game'. This is borne out by the fact that he achieved the very rare feat of playing a round in under his age when he was in his late 80s. There's a plaque in the clubhouse in honour of his achievement.

When I was about 12, I inherited an old set of golf clubs from him and a dozen or so golf balls from his vast collection, which were kept in an old suitcase under his bed. I would often practise in the school field opposite my home and I still possess his 8-iron. I later dabbled with the game and, whenever I told Dad I was off to play, he'd always come up with the same line: 'Don't forget your compass, Paul!'

As far as hobbies and domestic chores were concerned, my Dad was from a generation that thought nothing of tinkering with the car, doing the gardening or undertaking a few DIY jobs around the house, but apart from cleaning the car and changing the oil every now and then, and keeping the garden lawn in check, that was about it. When any serious horticultural tasks needed doing, his father would come over from Finchley on his small motorcycle on a Thursday afternoon. I looked forward immensely to these visits as Grandad would usually have a fresh bag of barley sugars in his pocket and, if I was patient and polite, I would receive one or two of them. If I did pluck up courage to ask for one, he'd reply: 'Presently, Paul, presently.'

Dad would sometimes pluck up courage and undertake a few menial gardening chores on a Sunday morning, and weeding the rockery was a favourite. I would often help him. After a few minutes Dad would be accosted by the inevitable lost motorist who would stop and ask us if this was the M1? The recently opened stretch from Bricket Wood to London was still a mystery to many weekend drivers and they would start to wonder if Mount Pleasant Lane was indeed the gateway to Mill Hill, Edgware and Golders Green. This was because they would follow the slip road from the A405 and, instead of following the signs to the motorway, would accidentally sweep round to the left. By the time they reached our bungalow we were sitting targets.

When the rockery was all neat and tidy we would concentrate on the back garden and in particular the patch of land behind the beech hedges, behind the (imaginary) football goal and (real) cricket crease. Once we were there and had been digging for a few minutes, Dad would say: 'We'll have a real go at the kitchen garden this year, Paul.' Every spring he'd repeat the line and every year the kitchen garden would never materialise. Normally, whatever duties were undertaken would generally be completed by mid-morning, giving us time to drive up the road and take in the football opposite the local social club, where Dad would meet up with his friends for a post-match, pre-Sunday-lunch light ale. I'd have a fizzy orange and munch away at the free chunks of cheese and crisps on offer at the bar.

Talking of kitchens, Dad very rarely cooked anything. When he did, it would invariably lead to disaster. He could handle Sugar Puffs or grated apple and a cup of tea for breakfast, and maybe herring roe on toast for tea, but that was about it. Mum wouldn't allow him to do anything more elaborate after he set fire to the kitchen one Saturday afternoon. Mum had gone on a keep-fit weekend with some of her friends, and Dad fancied scampi and chips. Unfortunately, he forgot to dry the scampi after rinsing them in the sink and, when tipping them into the boiling mass of fat, they caught fire and set the curtains alight. I was watching David

Coleman reading out the football results on *Grandstand* when the smell of smoke and burning nylon wafted through the hall and into the lounge, followed by the sound of Dad swearing at the top of his voice and beating the curtains with a tea towel: 'Christ almighty, what have I done?' I was too scared to leave the lounge and stayed put until the fire was extinguished, all the windows and back door had been opened and Dad had hastily removed the burnt curtains, putting them in the outside dustbin. Perhaps he thought Mum wouldn't notice that her kitchen curtains had gone missing? We had herring roe on toast for tea and Mum soon had a new set of kitchen curtains. Dad received strict instructions to never attempt to cook again.

Alfred Bishop

My dad's father was born on 18 July 1887, in Lydbrook in the Forest of Dean, Gloucestershire. One of his parents was Welsh, which made my dad one-quarter Welsh and gave me one-eighth Welsh or Celtic blood. In Michael Hurd's book, *Immortal Hour*, the biography of the English composer, Rutland Boughton (whose mother was born Grace Martha Bishop), he states: 'It is from the Bishops, the fine-boned Celtic Bishops, that Rutland Boughton inherited his musical gifts.' So it seems likely that Grace Bishop was a great-aunt (or possibly great-great-aunt) to my grandfather, as she is known to have had two nephews named John and Francis. Grace Bishop had a brother, Charles, who was a schoolteacher in Lydbrook, so there is a clear Forest of Dean connection. Her father, Francis, is described as a 'cheerful and contented old man', just like our grandfather. Soon after the end of the Great War in 1918, Alfred left Gloucestershire to seek work in London. When looking for a suitable place to live, he started in central London and found what appeared to be nice accommodation. He placed his suitcase on the floor and started chatting to the owner of the house. Before he could say a word the lady advised him to keep an eye on the case as it might get stolen. He left immediately and looked elsewhere, eventually finding a safer and more attractive place to raise his family in Finchley.

Rutland Boughton was a fan of Richard Wagner and is remembered for his attempt to create an 'English Bayreuth' at Glastonbury, where he established the first series of Glastonbury Festivals that ran with enormous success from 1914 until 1926. In 1978, on my first trip to Germany with my football club, St Albans Wanderers, I was taken to the Bayreuth Festival by my host, Alfred Bolian, and his family. Although not an opera or classical music fan, I remember it being a particularly special and important occasion, full of pride and nostalgia for the Germans – rather like the Last Night of the Proms is to us.

CHAPTER 2

Johnny Haynes

ON 25 November 1953, Hungary – the team ranked number one in the world – visited Wembley to play England in a game that became known as the 'Match of the Century'. England went into the encounter confident that they would preserve their unbeaten home record. At the end of a torrid 90 minutes they left the pitch beaten, bewildered and humiliated, after Hungary won 6-3. However, it wasn't just the scoreline that hurt; it was also the manner of the defeat. The performance, formation and tactical skill of the Hungarians were a wake-up call and would eventually change the way the game was played. The FA had created a climate of complacency, convinced that, having invented the game, all the players had to do was turn up and the opposition would be beaten.

On that day they were taught a harsh lesson. Hungary played a brand of 'total' football 20 years before Holland and – with over half the team coming from the state-sponsored army team, Honved – they were fitter, faster and tactically superior. England's pedestrian defence couldn't cope with deep-lying centre-forward Nandor Hidegkuti who hit a hat-trick. Skipper Ferenc Puskas was a revelation, running the game as well as chipping in with two goals; the first the famous 'drag-back' and left-foot finish that totally bemused England captain Billy Wright.

Wright recalls noticing the strange footwear worn by the Hungarians: 'When we walked out at Wembley I noticed that the Hungarians had on these strange, lightweight boots, cut away like slippers under the ankle bone. I turned to big Stan Mortensen and said, 'We should be alright here, Stan, they haven't got the proper kit.' Within a few months Surrey cricketer and London sports shop owner Stuart Surridge would be importing similar footwear from the West German supplier Adidas.

A young Malcolm Allison was a ball boy at the game and remembers the comments of one of his colleagues as they watched the Hungarians warm up. 'He was making fun of Puskas saying something like "we won't have any trouble today, judging by that fat little fellow". I wasn't too sure as he seemed to have pretty good technique and was pinging the ball around nonchalantly with that left foot of his.'

Pertinently, *The Guardian*'s report of the game was representative of the impact that Hungary's style of play had made: 'The English team was competent by British standards except at inside-forward, but on the evidence of this afternoon this standard will no longer be good enough for England to retain her position in the high places of the football world. The essential difference lay in attack, where none of the English forwards except Matthews approached the speed, ball control and positional play of the Hungarians.'

Six members of the England team – defenders Alf Ramsey, Bill Eckersley and Harry Johnston, and forwards

George Robb, Ernie Taylor and Stan Mortensen – never played for the national team again. But the FA were simply papering over the cracks, naively believing the Hungary defeat had been a one-off. They were sadly mistaken. A return game in Hungary the following spring ended 7-1 in the hosts' favour.

The time was right for change. The time was right for Johnny Haynes to make his international entrance.

Johnny Haynes was born in Kentish Town, north London, in 1934 and supported Arsenal as a boy. He looked set to sign for them or their near neighbours Tottenham Hotspur, as both clubs wanted him. However, his best friend and former England schoolboy international colleague Trevor 'Tosh' Chamberlain had joined Fulham the year before and told Haynes what a marvellous club it was. As a result he signed for them as a 15-year-old amateur in 1950 and made his senior debut, aged 18, on Boxing Day 1952 in the Second Division home game against Southampton.

Haynes first played for England at the age of 19 in October 1954, scoring a goal and setting up another for fellow debutant Don Revie in a 2-0 victory over Northern Ireland in Belfast. He was rewarded by being dropped along with Revie and six other players! Although England were managed by Walter Winterbottom, the team was picked by a group of selectors led by the then Chelsea chairman, Joe Mears, who was later to become chairman of the FA. It was to be a temporary blip and Haynes went on to play 56 games for England, 22 of them as captain.

So just how good a player was Johnny Haynes? And was he worth the hefty 1961 wage of £100 a week, the modern equivalent of £2,240, that Fulham paid him?

Johnny Haynes: 'I think I had a lot more to offer than just being the first £100-a-week footballer.'

He wasn't alone. Former England team-mate Jimmy Armfield described Haynes as being 'a midfield genius who had the eye and the skill to exploit any gap that any opposing defence might offer'. And the best English goalscorer of the day, Jimmy Greaves, certainly appreciated Haynes's ability to find the perfect pass: 'I thought "Haynesey" was a wonderful footballer, he completely dominated the midfield. I've never seen a better passer of the ball. One of his great assets was he always looked for the difficult through ball, which I, being a goalscorer, loved; I was on to them like a flash. He trusted his ability, he trusted his vision, he trusted his judgement and there was no one else in his class as a passer of the ball.'

Greaves also recalls a memorable match in the build-up to the 1962 World Cup finals in Chile when England travelled to Rome to take on Italy in a 'friendly': 'We were not in the game and 2-1 down when, with only a couple of minutes remaining, I ran over to take a throw-in only for me to see Omar Sivori approaching me. Well he was known to come up close as if to touch your face only to poke you in the eye so I took the throw quickly and the ball was crossed in and Gerry Hitchens hit the equaliser. We all thought we're out of jail! But then with seconds remaining, and the crowd very unhappy, Jimmy Armfield knocked the ball to Haynesey who shot and the goalkeeper parried it to yours truly, thank you very much, and the referee blew his whistle. So Haynesey decides to do a lap of honour, oh my God … there was everything coming over, rubble coming over the fence and the verbal abuse! Haynesey adored it but really we should have run off the pitch as quickly as possible. But a lap of honour while Rome burned for the second time? I would say that was the pinnacle of his international career. He was a great player and a great captain.'

Fulham and England colleague Sir Bobby Robson, who later went on to manage the club – as well as Ipswich Town, England, PSV Eindhoven, Sporting Lisbon, Porto, Barcelona and his beloved Newcastle – was well qualified to recognise a good footballer when he saw one: 'Johnny Haynes was a great player. I'm not saying he was a good player, or a very good player. He was a great player and there's a difference. He was a master of the pass; that was his quality, long or short. He had the great idea about penetration of the pass. Johnny could play the ace-in-the-hole pass and his selection was exquisite, it was always spot on. He always knew which was the best pass to give, and that's a star.'

Jimmy Hill played with Haynes many times for Fulham: 'Fulham knew how lucky they were to have him. He chose to come to the family club beside the Thames as we had some extraordinary talent there. Apart from Johnny we had Bobby Robson, Bedford Jezzard, Bill Dodgin, Frank Osborne as manager and comedian Tommy Trinder as chairman. Off the field it really was fun, but on it Johnny could be a miserable so-and-so and didn't suffer fools gladly, and if one of his comrades was responsible for losing the ball he would let him know he wasn't pleased. If he made a mistake he was twice as vile!'

Jimmy Armfield agreed: 'Jimmy Greaves got it absolutely right by saying Haynes trusted his own ability. The only trouble for us England and Fulham colleagues was that he expected all of us to reach the same perfection. If I made a mistake I'd automatically look at Johnny who would be glaring at me with his hand on his hip.'

Haynes's successor as England captain, Bobby Moore, said of him: 'Once you got used to watching that perfection you realised the rest of the secret. John was always available, always hungry for the ball, always wanting to play. I loved watching the player. Later I learnt to love the man.'

Another World Cup winner and Fulham team-mate, George Cohen: 'I have a hundred individual memories of the beauty of John's play. One stands out for the sheer perfection of his skill. It was a charity match which, but for that one second, has faded completely from my memory. The ball came to him at speed on a wet, slippery surface but with the slightest of adjustments, one that was almost imperceptible, he played it inside the full-back and into the path of an on-running winger. I looked at our coach Dave Sexton on the bench and he caught my glance and shook his head as if to say 'fantastic'. Haynes could give you goosebumps on a wet night in a match that didn't matter.'

On the day of Haynes's death, Alan Mullery, another ex-Fulham and England player, paid the following tribute: 'He was the only reason I went to Fulham as a young boy of 15 leaving school. He was my hero, the captain of England and Fulham. The word 'great' rolls off the tongue quite easily these days but he really was. He was the best passer of a ball I have ever seen – I don't know anyone who could pass a ball as accurately. Anyone who saw him will know what a great player he was.'

And last, but by no means least, Pelé, acknowledged by most to be the game's greatest -ever player, said: 'I've never seen a better passer of the ball than Johnny Haynes.'

In August 1962, the sports car in which Haynes was returning to his Blackpool hotel was blown by a gust of wind into the path of another vehicle. Haynes broke bones in both feet and badly injured a knee. He missed almost a season and, when he returned to the Fulham side, he was never the same player. He was only 27, and expected to lead England in the 1966 World Cup; but he was never again selected for the national team.

Haynes retired from football in 1970. A couple of years before that, he played in a charity game just outside Bricket Wood. My dad must have been told about the game by one of his pals in the pub and he once again invited me to come along and watch the game with him. It was a low-key Sunday morning match with just a handful of spectators. Haynes was majestic and the perfect gentleman. I was standing on the sideline when the ball came out of the sky and went off for a throw. I managed to control it with one touch before Haynes arrived to take the throw. After picking up the ball, he found the time to praise me: 'Well trapped, son.' Just three words, but for a 13-year-old football-mad boy it meant the world and I've never forgotten it.

Both Jimmy Hill and Alan Mullery speak fondly of their time at Fulham and I can remember my grandfather, Fred Hockey, who was originally from north London with Arsenal and Spurs on his doorstep, choosing Fulham as his team. My dad also had a soft spot for them and, rather like Billy Connolly used to think his local side were called Partick Thistle Nil, Dad always called them Poor Old Fulham! During the early and mid-60s they were constantly fighting off relegation to the Second Division until the inevitable occurred in the 1967/68 season when they went down. Worse was to come the following season when they were relegated to the Third Division. Poor old Fulham indeed. Like most football clubs they were fallible and often flattered to deceive, but they were well loved by football fans in general. Terry McCann, actor Dennis Waterman's character in the long-running 1980s ITV comedy drama *Minder*, was a Fulham fan and that can't be bad, especially as in real life Waterman supports near neighbours Chelsea. It's nice to report that Fulham have just been promoted to the Premier League, beating west London neighbours Brentford in the play-off final.

CHAPTER 3
The Early Days

THE WATFORD team that played against Coventry was managed by former Tottenham and Swansea left-half Ron Burgess and included goalkeeper Dave Underwood, defenders Bobby Bell, Ken Nicholas, Terry Mancini and Vince McNeice, with Tommy Harmer, Freddie Bunce and Sammy Chung in attack.

Welshman Burgess spent four years in charge at Vicarage Road and had a great start in the 1959/60 season, gaining promotion to Division Three. The following season he almost did it again, but by the time Coventry arrived he was under pressure. His relationship with the fans had been on the slide since he sold star striker and fans' favourite Cliff Holton to Northampton Town in 1961. When the board failed to back him, he was replaced by Bill McGarry at the start of the 1963/64 season.

Two of the team that played against Coventry – goalkeeper Dave Underwood and full-back Bobby Bell – were familiar to me in the immediate years following the game. Both visited

Bricket Wood on occasions. Underwood used to pick up his paper from Fred Stock's newsagents in Old Watford Road and my dad introduced me to him. He was big and bubbly with a battered face and a mass of curly hair – a natural showman. Bell was Watford's hardman who occasionally played on Sunday mornings for Bricket Wood Social Club's Acorn side.

Dave Underwood

Dave Underwood was born in London in 1928 and started his professional football career in 1949 with Queens Park Rangers before signing for Watford in 1952. In all, he had three spells at Vicarage Road, with a three-year spell as Liverpool's stopper from 1953 until 1956 sandwiched between. Underwood, who was a boxer in his army days, was known as the dressing-room comedian. When he signed for Liverpool their manager, Don Welsh, claimed Underwood was 'the most promising young goalkeeper in football'. Underwood started the 1954/55 season as first choice but after playing 26 consecutive league and cup games lost his place before the end of the season. He was incensed and demanded to be put on the transfer list. His wish was granted and he returned to Watford, then in the Third Division South, in July 1956. Although always a popular figure at the club, Underwood played part-time as he was also working for a local haulage contractor at the time. As a result he then spent three seasons at non-league Dartford before once again returning to Watford in 1960. Underwood's performances impressed and he was voted Watford's Player of the Year in 1962 and landed a move to First Division Fulham.

In 1977 Underwood was appointed chairman of Barnet until 1982. During his time there he signed Jimmy Greaves, who later thanked Underwood for helping him in his fight to overcome alcohol addiction. Dave Underwood passed away in January 1989.

Bobby Bell

Bobby Bell was born in Ayr on 16 September 1934 and played in Scottish Junior Football for Whitletts Victoria, and also for the British Army during his national service. Bell turned professional in August 1954 when he signed for Falkirk. Manager Bob Shankly selected Bell for one league game, before releasing him on a free transfer at the end of the 1955/56 season. Former Watford manager Neil McBain signed Bell when he was managing Ayr, and when McBain rejoined Watford in August 1956, he signed several former Ayr players, including Bell.

Bell became a regular Watford first-team player and, along with Cliff Holton, helped the club gain promotion to the Third Division in 1959/60, for the first time in our history. Watford achieved a fourth-placed league finish in 1961, and third place in 1964. The arrival of player-manager Ken Furphy in 1964 signalled the end of Bell's Watford career; Furphy was also a full-back, and selected himself in preference to Bell. After spending most of the 1964/65 season in Watford's reserves, Bell joined non-league Wealdstone on a free transfer in July 1965.

In the late 60s Bell would occasionally turn out on Sunday mornings for Bricket Wood Social Club's Acorn team. At that time my dad was fond of a couple of lunchtime ales in the club, and the first time I accompanied him to watch Acorn was memorable. I remember most of the local spectators, used to Bell's robust and at times brutal tackling, were waiting in anticipation of a typical crunching challenge. Sure enough, midway through the first half, the opposition's young winger knocked the ball past Bobby and, full of confidence, started to skip past the struggling Scot. He didn't have a chance. Bobby's late challenge ended up with the unfortunate winger being 'taken out' and dumped some five yards or so off the pitch. Much ironic chuckling from the locals followed as the battered boy was helped back to the changing rooms ...

Following his retirement from professional football, Bell worked for aircraft engine manufacturer Rolls Royce in Leavesden, just outside Watford. He played for their football team, and managed them from 1979 until 1981. He later coached Leverstock Green and Mill End, and managed in Sunday league football in the 1990s. Bell died in 2007.

Cliff Holton – The Idol of Vicarage Road

There are three Watford players from the early to mid-60s who, all these years later, remain special to me. Although I never saw Cliff Holton play, his legend lives on some 25 years after his death. Cliff had two spells at Watford and, prior to his arrival in 1958, had already become a hero at First Division Arsenal, helping them reach the FA Cup Final in 1952 and win the league title the following season with 22 goals in all, 19 of them in the league.

A big, powerful, two-footed centre-forward, Holton was the perfect striker, but he was also versatile, playing in midfield and at centre-half too. In 207 games for the Gunners, he scored an impressive 88 goals and was considered unlucky not to be capped by England. Then, in 1958, Watford got lucky and signed him for a Division Four record fee of £10,000. At the time, the arrival of the 29-year-old striker was greeted by fans with disbelief, shock and finally delight. Holton spent three seasons with the Hornets, mostly at centre-forward. He formed a successful partnership with Dennis Uphill, scoring a club record 48 goals in 1959/60, which also saw the club promoted to the Third Division. In that spell Holton scored 84 goals in 120 appearances before being controversially sold to Northampton Town in 1961. Manager Ron Burgess had some disagreements with Holton and, foolishly believing the club would be better off without him, persuaded the board to sell him. Next was a three-year stint at Crystal Palace, before he returned to Vicarage Road for the 1965/66 season.

Cliff Holton's departure from Vicarage Road in the late summer of 1961 caused an uproar – especially with supporters, who turned against Burgess. This ultimately resulted in the manager getting the sack, to be replaced by Bill McGarry. Holton's shadow remained over the club for a decade. Fifteen years later, when Jim Bonser resigned as chairman, he was still trying to justify that transfer, which disillusioned a generation of Vicarage Road regulars. When he stepped down he finally admitted what all the fans had known 15 years earlier: 'We got rid of the wrong man.' Holton went on to score a club record 36 goals in 1961/62, achieving the rare feat of holding the all-time record for goals in a season at two different clubs. Holton later said that he retained a particular affinity for Watford, more so than for Arsenal where he spent the greater part of his career. 'I loved scoring goals and loved the cheers they brought,' he said. 'And I loved to have 26,000 people chanting "we want Cliff". It was something very special in my life.'

I believe young sports fans from any generation have an affinity with players who in some way stand out and are different from the crowd. I have always admired mavericks and have already mentioned my hero-worship of Denis Law, whose showmanship, mannerisms and arrogance appealed to me. It was the same with tennis. I used to hurry home from school to catch live Wimbledon coverage on the TV, and Torben Ulrich was one of my favourite players. Ulrich was an elegant left-handed Danish player, who looked like a hippy before hippies were 'hip', with long blond hair held in place by a bright bandana. This was in the mid-60s and I had never seen a man with long hair, let alone a bandana! He was also a writer, artist, filmmaker and jazz enthusiast. Compared with the clean-cut Brits, Aussies and Americans of that era, he was a breath of fresh air. A few years later the supremely gifted but temperamental Romanian gypsy, Ilie Nastase, took over his mantle. To put it simply, Ulrich and Nastase not only looked different, but played the game differently too.

Sammy Chung

Cyril 'Sammy' Chung looked different and his surname sounded different. Sammy was born in Oxfordshire on 16 July 1932. His father was Chinese and his mother English. After spells with Abingdon Town, Headington United, Reading and Norwich City, he moved to Watford for the 1957/58 season. Under manager Neil McBain, the side were relegated to the Fourth Division. The Hornets secured a return to the Third Division with promotion in 1959/60 and narrowly missed out on promotion to the second tier in 1960/61 and 1963/64. Chung played 242 times for Watford and scored 24 goals.

Chung gained his first coaching experience while still a player at Watford, under manager Bill McGarry. When McGarry left to become manager of Ipswich Town, he took

Chung with him as assistant. At Ipswich they won promotion to the First Division as champions in 1968. Following a short period as manager of Swedish side IFK Västerås, he returned to join Bill McGarry, now at Wolverhampton Wanderers, as his assistant. As part of the management team, they guided Wolves to victory in the 1974 League Cup. The club were relegated in 1976 and McGarry departed, leaving Chung to be appointed manager.

After a period coaching in the United Arab Emirates, Chung returned to England in 1985 as assistant manager to Mick Mills at Stoke City. Spells at Blackburn Rovers, Tamworth and Doncaster Rovers followed before he was appointed director of football in Barbados in 1999. In 2005, he joined the coaching staff at Minehead. After retiring from football, Chung worked in a children's home. He now lives in Somerset.

Ken Furphy

Ken Furphy was the first truly successful manager Watford had. Before Furphy the club were stuck like glue in the Third Division. Following his arrival as player-manager in 1964, Furphy, with a meagre budget, patiently built a side around such seasoned stalwarts as Keith Eddy, Tom Walley and Terry Garbett. Then, with the addition of Barry Endean, signed in late 1968, Furphy achieved what many of the older fans thought was impossible: he took the club to the promised land of Division Two, in April 1969. I remember the run-in was tense, with Watford vying with Swindon, Luton and Plymouth for the promotion places. When Swindon clocked up four consecutive wins at the end of February, they had a four-point lead. When an interviewer pointed out to the

Watford manager that his side had two games in hand, Furphy was at his most philosophical, replying: 'Yes, but games in hand are not necessarily games won.' For many years after, games in hand were known as 'Furphys' in our house. Five years after Furphy left to manage Blackburn, the club were back in Division Four.

Looking back, Furphy had some of Jimmy Hill's innovative spark. His televised team talk, broadcast on *Grandstand* and introduced by David Coleman, before the fourth-round FA Cup tie against Manchester United at Old Trafford, was a first. It was a masterful piece of PR, sending out a positive message to players, fans, the opposition and football in general. Indeed Coleman described Furphy as 'one of the best young managers in the game today'.

To say Furphy's talk is thorough doesn't do it justice. His instructions on how to handle George Best are a good example. He tells Tom Walley to man-mark Best, but only to go in and 'have a bite' when both Keith Eddy and Dixie Hale are covering him. He also briefs Terry Garbett on the unenviable task of marking Bobby Charlton. Garbett, an underrated player in my opinion, did a great job, keeping Charlton quiet for large parts of the game.

It must be said that most of the players listening to Furphy's pearls of wisdom look like bored schoolchildren who can't wait for the end-of-class bell to ring. For instance, Barry Endean is shown chewing his tie nervously and one player at the back almost disappears behind a thick cloud of cigarette smoke! But it worked. The team were certainly 'up for it' once the game got underway, with Stewart Scullion's right-foot rocket from almost 30 yards into the top corner of Jimmy Rimmer's goal coming after just two minutes. Mike Walker in Watford's goal had a fine match up until the hour mark, when he bumped into Johnny Williams and dropped the ball into the path of Denis Law. 'The King' duly equalised. Law had the last laugh as well, scoring both goals in the replay on an ice rink of a pitch at the Vic just over a week later.

Furphy's man-management skills came to the fore again the following season, when the team again punched above their weight and reached the semi-finals of the FA Cup. On the way to that last-four encounter against eventual winners Chelsea at White Hart Lane, Watford knocked out both Liverpool and Stoke City. The Liverpool game was really special; an outstanding team performance on a 'suet pudding' of a pitch at Vicarage Road, with Ray Lugg outstanding. I was in my usual position, standing on 'the bend' – the cindered area between the Rookery and the Shrodells Stand – and got a perfect view of Barry Endean's winning header past Tommy Lawrence.

Born in Stockton-on-Tees in 1931, Ken Furphy's playing career began in 1953 as a full-back at nearby Darlington, before he went west to play for Workington nine years later. It wasn't to be the only time Furphy travelled west. Whilst there, he met the Scottish-born centre-half, George Aitken. Aitken retired from playing in 1960 to become trainer at Workington, initially for Joe Harvey and then under Furphy. When the latter left to manage Watford, he took Aitken along as his assistant. They, along with the irrepressible and charismatic physio Pat Molloy, made a good and well-balanced management team.

Furphy made several shrewd signings in his first couple of years at Watford, including Keith Eddy from Barrow and Terry Garbett from Middlesbrough. Both, like Furphy, were northerners – Eddy was actually born in Barrow-in-Furness, and Garbett in Lanchester, near Durham – and wherever Furphy went, these two followed. Eddy, a stylish half-back, soon became skipper and a trusted penalty taker too. I don't recall him ever missing from the spot, and he was known as Eddy Pen in our house, because this is how his name often appeared in the results sections of the national press, as well as the local *Watford Observer* and *Evening Echo*.

Ray Lugg was another of Furphy's signings. Again a northerner, this time from Jarrow, Lugg was signed, like Garbett, from Middlesbrough, for a paltry £8,000. Before the Liverpool game Bill Shankly saw Lugg play at Bristol Rovers and said he was 'a player with composure and class'. Furphy said after the game: 'I reckon Ray is worth ten times that amount today.' However, for some reason Lugg couldn't repeat that type of performance regularly and he was sold to Plymouth Argyle two years later. Eddy was sold to Sheffield United in 1972, a year before Furphy joined as manager, and then joined him at New York Cosmos in 1976.

Terry Garbett was my favourite Watford player; our answer to Johnny Haynes – always looking for that special pass. He also chipped in an impressive 46 goals from 200 appearances. Garbett followed Furphy to Blackburn Rovers, Sheffield United and then to New York Cosmos in the North American Soccer League (NASL) in 1976.

Although Furphy had gained a fine reputation for managing home-grown players, many of them from familiar backgrounds to his own, he must have found it harder handling players like the Brazilians Pelé and Carlos Alberto as well as West Germany's Franz Beckenbauer. With hindsight, Furphy probably regrets the first words he said to Pelé: 'I'm going to treat you just like any of the other players, so don't expect anything special.' Pelé was probably unused to this and, rumour has it, he was instrumental in getting Furphy the sack after just one season in charge. Pelé was later apologetic, saying he liked and admired Furphy and regretted his actions.

I am sure Furphy will always be remembered fondly by Watford fans. He was one of the first of the new breed of young tracksuited bosses; a hard-working tactician, fond of compiling lengthy dossiers. He was, like Graham Taylor, a good and friendly communicator with the media and keen on forming strong links with fans and the local community. Crucially, he was used to working on a financial shoestring during the early part of his managerial career and the trip 'across the pond' to the razzamatazz of American soccer and big egos may have been a journey too far. But the road from Stockton-on-Tees to New York was still something special.

Meanwhile Dad's job meant he was also doing a bit of travelling, as a salesman with London-based electrical wholesaler JJ Eastick. He was always an early riser and out on the road by 7.30 at the latest. Although not a workaholic, he didn't really fancy family holidays, and my mum had to nag him to take a week off during the school holidays for the sake of us children.

The first holiday I can remember was in 1961 when we visited Tredegar in south Wales to pay homage to Dad's hero, Nye Bevan. I'd like to say I can recall walking around Tredegar hand in hand with Dad visiting the mine where the great man worked, as well as the social clubs, pubs and souvenir shops selling mugs, ashtrays and postcards with Nye's smiling face on them. But I can't. All I can actually remember is being scared to death by the traditional costumes the women wore, which made them look like witches. I had nightmares about them for years after!

I also have fond memories of a holiday we spent in Topsham, Devon, in 1962. We were staying in a pretty good hotel and the waiter did a passable impression of the singer Frank Ifield, who had a massive number-one hit at the time called 'I Remember You'. When Australian-born Ifield would sing the chorus he'd introduce some yodelling whenever the word 'you' came up, and the waiter's enthusiasm, combined with his confident singing voice and volume, meant all the guests could hear him coming from almost anywhere in the establishment.

The hotel was close to the beach, so there was swimming, beach cricket and sandcastles to enjoy. Of the three, beach cricket proved to be the safest. Swimming was never something any of the family were interested in, and on this holiday sandcastles proved to be particularly unpleasant and painful for me. Arriving at the beach one morning, I had planned to build several castles, a moat and then decorate them with hundreds of shells; nothing too grand! For this elaborate piece of sand art to work, I would need some help from Dad, who was 50 yards away near the cliffs, talking with my Mum and brother Laurie. I called out several times, each time becoming more and more agitated and each time bringing my new wooden and metal spade (no plastic in those days, unfortunately) down hard into the sand. Seeing there was still no sign of Dad, I shouted out a final time, bringing the spade down on my big toe. My screams soon got Dad's attention and he was by my side in a flash, giving me a right telling-off as he guided me into the sea to wash away the blood. I'm sure there must be a moral to this tale, but I'm not sure what it is. What I do know is that I've still got the scar and the sandcastles never got built.

The 1964 holiday to Butlin's Minehead was unforgettable as the whole family were laid low with tummy bugs for the week after a bout of gastroenteritis swept through the place. Lucky we didn't book for a fortnight. There was a more pleasant visit to the Forest of Dean, where Grandad Bishop was born, and nearby Ross-on-Wye the following year.

Back in Bricket Wood, Mum was often keen to get me out of the house on Saturday mornings. She probably wanted the house free to do the weekly clean-up. Dad often worked on Saturday mornings and Laurie was nearly always at school until lunchtime. As this was before I was old enough to attend regular football matches on my own or with my friends, I was the only potential problem. My dad had a cunning plan. Every three or four weeks he had to visit head office in Clerkenwell, central London, and when this happened, guess who accompanied him? This was great for me as I always enjoyed family car trips, especially as Dad's car at that time seemed unusual to me. It was a light-blue Simca Aronde P60. I have no idea why he changed from his trusty Vauxhall Victor, especially as he wasn't particularly enamoured with the French. I think this stemmed from the time he was shot at by local snipers whilst driving his tank through rural France during the war.

When we arrived at the office I was introduced to some of the staff, including the firm's accounts lady, Rene Pring, who always made a fuss of me. Dad would make me feel very important by saying something like: 'This is Paul and he's come along today to give me a hand.' This would make me feel really special and I would stand there and take a deep breath to help me keep calm. It was then that I caught the unforgettable smell of cardboard. The office was full of stock and the boxes were stacked to the ceiling in a storeroom at the back. Dad would then chat to a few of his colleagues before it would be time to go. I should think we were only there an hour or so, but it would give my mum enough time to do the hoovering and ironing. It also gave us ample time to have some lunch in one of my dad's favourite Italian restaurants. These were usually in the Borehamwood/Elstree area.

This was a great treat and I quickly became used to Dad's favourite dish, minestrone soup. It would always be accompanied by him saying: 'If you go to an Italian restaurant, Paul, you must have minestrone.' I always remembered this valuable piece of culinary advice and now pass it on to my own children every chance I get. This is not often, as my wife is from Galicia in north-west Spain, so pulpo Gallego, croquetas, tortilla and caldo Gallego get the children's vote most of the time. Mine too, if I'm honest. But my son Harry likes pasta, so if we do find ourselves in an Italian establishment, the minestrone will always get my vote.

CHAPTER 4

Cuffley Camp, 1966 and All That

UP UNTIL September 1964 my burgeoning sporting career had been confined to football practice, when the weather was dry, and cricket, tennis and badminton matches against my older brother Laurie in spring and summer. All took place in the back garden at 41 Mount Pleasant Lane, Bricket Wood. The garden was a good size and I soon became accustomed to solo soccer games with the help of the garage brick wall, which I used to play one-twos off. The wall was also a useful tennis opponent during Wimbledon fortnight. 'Clarence' the willow tree took up a fair proportion of the corner of the garden, next to the swing and near my imaginary goal – no Samba plastic goals and nets in those days, folks!

Cricket matches against my brother were usually a mix of entertainment, arguments and humour. I was often England and Laurie represented the West Indies. The length of the garden lawn was less than 22 yards, but for me, aged seven or so, it was plenty big enough. I must mention now that there were a couple of design faults with the garden. At the bowler's end – sometimes the Nursery End, at other times the Kirkstall Lane End – there were tiles angled upwards that meant a low straight drive would be very risky as the ball would rise up off the tiles and hit either my parents' bedroom window or the windows of the spare room. This meant that anything harder than a tennis ball could be destructive and lead to disaster and a severe telling-off. Even so, on a dampish pitch the tennis ball was often heavy enough to cause a spectacular smashing of glass. The concrete area was known as crazy paving. This was appropriate as our cricket games were often crazy affairs, as I'll explain.

The other problem at the bowler's end became evident when Laurie adopted the guise of one of the 'Windies' fast bowlers – either Wes Hall or Charlie Griffith. To accommodate their 30 or 40-yard run-up, Laurie needed to start somewhere at the end of the driveway, near the gate, rendering him invisible until he appeared level with the back of the bungalow. He would then skilfully negotiate the two concrete steps and continue on to the lawn before releasing the ball.

When in a mischievous mood, my brother would often lengthen his run-up so that he started 30 or so yards down the road, near Miss Brice's grocery shop, leaving me waiting at the crease unsure when he would arrive. I sometimes thought he had stopped off at the shop for some sweets, he took so long! The longer the run-up the longer I had to wait. Sometimes the tension was too much and I would have to run down to check on when Wes or Charlie would arrive. Laurie would sometimes be kind enough to give me a clue as to when he would arrive at the crease by singing a popular cricket calypso of that time:

Charlie Griffith and Wesley Hall, the fastest bowlers of the cricket ball.

Wes he bowl and the ball go through, Charlie bowl and the air turn blue!

Cricket lovely cricket, cricket lovely cricket, cricket lovely cricket, cricket lovely cricket.

Although our neighbours on one side were a friendly family with young children, the elderly couple on the other side, Wally and Marge, were childless, humourless and what little love they had was devoted to their garden. Although Laurie and I loved our garden, flowers, herbs and shrubs were nowhere near as important as football, cricket and tennis. Although we only had one plastic football, we needed to have a good supply of tennis balls as Wally and Marge would often take weeks to throw them back! Marge rarely talked to us, mainly restricting herself to a mean scowl every now and then. But she did say something to us once over the garden fence that continues to confuse and concern me to this day: 'Be careful with those balls, you know I have trouble with my head.' Was it headaches or migraines or something worse? Alas, we will never know.

Wally could also be a pain. He once complained to my dad, saying his electric shaver interfered with their TV signal and could he possibly shave sometime before the evening news or maybe after 7pm. A few years later Marge passed away and Rose Anthony, a widow from down the road, moved in only to die a year or so later. When learning of Rose's demise, dad said: 'Christ knows what he does to them?'

As well as reenacting various Test matches, Laurie and I once tried to reproduce a goal scored by Nottingham Forest forward Ian Storey-Moore. It was the third goal against Everton in an FA Cup tie in 1966. The goal involved Storey-Moore having his first shot blocked by a defender, only to have his follow-up shot parried by the goalkeeper. His third attempted header rebounded off the bar to him and he headed it in. It proved to be a challenge for us, especially as we didn't have a goal, let alone a crossbar. I seem to remember us constructing one solely for this, using some of Dad's pieces of spare timber and an old fence post nailed and taped on top for the crossbar.

In September 1964 I enjoyed my first experience of competitive football. I was chosen for the Mount Pleasant Lane (MPL) school side, at the age of nine. The PE teacher, Mr Bowyer, picked me at right-back, a position I was to play in many times over the next 30 years. I was so proud to wear the school colours of yellow and blue halved shirts and white shorts and socks, and as the youngest member of the team I felt I acquitted myself quite well. The main problem, not uncommon in those days, was that I had trouble kicking the heavy leather and laced ball. On a wet and muddy day I had difficulty shifting the bloody thing more than a few yards unless I had the good fortune and opportunity to kick it first time, and then it would go a tad further. Luckily, finding a team-mate wasn't a priority for a defender back then; distance was the thing – at least that was my philosophy!

One aspect of the game I became good at was helping out our goalkeeper, Keith Bunker, from time to time. Keith was one of the smallest lads in the team, so found himself in goal and sometimes struggled in the frequent goalmouth melees that would take place. I would position myself near the goal line and became a specialist in making last-ditch off-the-line clearances. Other players I can remember from that team were

Howard Pay, Keith Slaney, Steve Hobbs, Eugene McCool, Paul Hunt, Alan Paradise and Barry Davidson. Barry was our main goalscorer and, living two or three miles away in Park Street, would get a lift to and from school with the music teacher, Mrs Booth.

By the time that first year of school football was coming to an end, I was hooked on the game. Even though the school was opposite our home, I would still get up at 7.20am in the spring and summer months to drink a quick cup of tea made by Dad, before he left for work. Cereals followed and I would then cross the road to be first at school and often met the caretaker's assistant, John, in his office for a drink of milk or bottled orange juice which the milkman would have just delivered. I'd be on the playing fields with my plastic football by 7.45, waiting for some of my footballing friends to arrive for a five or six-a-side game on the grass. Heaven!

A few lessons and break would get in the way until the serious stuff – in the shape of another match – would be arranged straight after lunch. It was around this time that the infamous 'Lunchgate' incident happened. Over a period of a few weeks, myself and some friends devised a prank that involved ordering double portions of whatever was on the menu. It was usually spam fritters with mashed potatoes, or beef stew with mashed potatoes, or maybe liver with mashed potatoes – anything as long as we had mashed potatoes on the plate. Gradually, we would order more and more food and eat less and less. When finished we had to empty our leftovers, which by this stage would be about a foot high, into the slop bin. Oh what fun we had!

Alas, our glee was short-lived; the catering crew must have been spying on us! We were called, one by one, into the study of the headmaster, Mr T.G. Daniels. Mr Daniels was a dark-haired, short, stout Welshman who, as well as signing any school correspondence with his flamboyant signature, would greet us in his native tongue at assembly on St David's Day. As with most of our teachers he looked very old indeed, although he was probably only in his mid to late thirties. However old he was, he certainly didn't appear too happy as we showed him our mash mountains. He asked us individually what the reason was for leaving the mashed potato and each one of us came up with the same answer: 'It tastes like soap, sir.' He took it well but the game was over and we were told we were to order and eat a normal plateful of food in future or else!

I quite liked Mr Daniels, but I remember Dad wasn't too keen on him. Being a Welshman, like Nye Bevan, I thought this odd. But around this time the school were planning to build a new swimming pool, one of only a few in the county. Anyway, Mr Daniels had been pestering parents to help pay for the pool and this might not have gone down too well with Dad's socialist principles.

The following year, my last at MPL, was going to be special, but at the time I didn't know quite how special. My fix of school football alongside lessons continued until, with the end of term approaching, we were told we would be going to Cuffley Camp to celebrate the end of our primary school days. I'd experienced plenty of trips away with my parents – holidays to Dorset, Devon, Gloucestershire, Wales and Minehead – but I'd never been away on my own, so I was understandably excited – especially as the week at Butlin's Minehead the year before had been a disaster. A bad dose of food poisoning hit the holiday camp a couple of days after our arrival, so we were far from happy campers, spending more time sick in bed and the bathroom than at the knobbly knees and glamorous granny contests. We would refer to Butlin's as Colditz from then on.

Cuffley Camp has operated as an outdoor education centre in Hertfordshire for over 70 years. The first Outward Bound centre, at Aberdyfi in west Wales, was established during the Second World War, and from the 1950s onwards the number of camps grew rapidly across the country. The camp was situated in south-west Hertfordshire and was a truly magical place for any youngster to visit. We duly departed on 28 May for our week of fun in the sun.

Although I was never a cub or boy scout, the running of the camp seemed to be loosely based on the practices of Baden-Powell's Scout movement – but, thankfully, without the dib dib dibs and dob dob dobs. I remember there was some kind of a rota with a number of tasks that we had to take on. These included erecting our tent, making our beds and stuffing fresh straw into our pillowcases, as well as a bit of map-reading. I could manage all of these apart from the map-reading. To this day I have almost no sense of direction and back then I used to get lost whenever I was more than a few hundred yards from my home.

We also had to collect wood and water and prepare vegetables, with mashed potatoes again featuring prominently! We also had to keep everything, including ourselves, clean. The latter proved tricky as the showers were always freezing cold. But the weather was warm and sunny and there was plenty of time for games of football and softball, so I was a happy camper at last.

Evenings were really special as we would cook our own supper round the campfire, with a little help from Mr Bowyer.

I really enjoyed drinking cocoa for the first time. I had to take my own cutlery, plates and also a maroon-coloured drinking mug made out of Bakelite.

Bakelite was the first type of plastic and, as well as my mug, Laurie and I had a fantastic wireless in our bedroom that used to hum and light up when you switched it on. I used to have great fun operating the dial with the dexterity of a safe-cracker so I could listen to one of the pirate stations such as Radio Caroline or Luxembourg that were popular in the 60s. My mum was a big wireless fan, listening to the BBC's *Light Programme* throughout the day. She introduced me to ex-trumpeter and bandleader Jack Jackson's Saturday lunchtime show that was years ahead of its time. He would link records with comedy clips from the likes of *Steptoe and Son* and Tony Hancock. Earlier on Saturday mornings I would listen to Brian Matthew's *Saturday Club* programme in bed, trying to memorise the words to songs by The Beatles, Rolling Stones, Gerry and the Pacemakers and my secret sweetheart, Dusty Springfield. I would keep my head well under the covers so no one could hear me. We also had a marvellous Bakelite hairdryer that weighed a ton. All the family used it regularly and it lasted for many years. This was before built-in obsolescence became the norm. Bakelite eventually fell out of favour when it was discovered it contained formaldehyde and asbestos.

I returned home on 3 June, my birthday, to be told by my parents that I had been accepted at the new comprehensive secondary school, just a mile away in Garston, near Watford. Both my parents were originally hoping I would replicate Laurie's academic success and join him at St Albans School. There were two reasons why this was not possible. Firstly, the school played rugby and not football, and secondly, I wasn't clever enough, having failed the maths part of the entrance exam quite spectacularly.

Safe in the knowledge that I would soon be attending a football-playing school, I started preparing myself for the important business of supporting England in the forthcoming World Cup that England would be hosting for the first, and so far only, time. Our rather dour national manager, Alf Ramsey, had already predicted England skipper Bobby Moore would be lifting the cup at Wembley Stadium on 30 July before a small-time cockney thief, Edward Betchley, did the same when he stole it from an exhibition in Westminster Central Hall on 20 March. The nation held its breath for a week until David Corbett's pet dog, Pickles, sniffed it out and found it wrapped in an old newspaper under a hedge in the front garden of his south-east London home. The hound became a hero and Corbett became rich, receiving a reward of £6,000 some time later.

I was a little confused about all this talk about the missing cup as I had received it as a birthday present from my parents and had attempted to engrave the word 'England' at the base of the trophy with one of my mum's pins from her embroidery box. Alas I made a right mess with the 'E' and decided to go no further. I asked my dad if this would affect the value of the solid-gold cup, but he assured me that it wouldn't.

Despite Alf's prediction, I, along with most of the country, was not feeling quite as confident during the long build-up to the tournament. But I did have a new companion to share my anxiety with – World Cup Willie. The first-ever World Cup mascot, created by freelance illustrator Reg Hoye, was an instant hit with children and adults alike and was a serious summer rival to Esso's Tiger Tail, which promised to put a 'Tiger in the Tank' of my dad's recently purchased Ford Cortina GT.

Thanks mainly to the BBC, the 1966 World Cup didn't start until Monday, 11 July, a month or so later than previous tournaments. The reason for the unusually late scheduling was because 'Auntie' had already committed to cover Wimbledon, which ran between 20 June and 2 July, and the Open Golf Championship from 6 to 9 July.

The tournament was special for me as it was my first opportunity to watch top-class football on a more or less daily basis. OK, I didn't go to see any matches 'live' but, thanks to Dad's job, our telly was good and big enough for all of us to watch the games in glorious black and white. Even Mum would often join us in the front room and ask irritating questions like: 'Who's playing?' and 'What's the score?' I had caught a dose of 'World Cup fever' and to prove it watched *Goal!*, the official documentary film of the tournament shot in glorious colour, at a local cinema as soon as it was released.

There was no need for mum's second question because England's opening game against Uruguay was a deadly dull 0-0 draw at Wembley, where all of our games would be played. Uruguay played for a point from the start, with nine men at the back. Ramsey played with just one winger, Manchester United's John Connelly, with Jimmy Greaves and Roger Hunt up front. At the final whistle Uruguay celebrated their point as if they had won the trophy.

The second of England's three group games was against Mexico, five days later. Ramsey settled for the same formation, but with Southampton's Terry Paine replacing Connelly. Not long into the game, the crowd started chanting, 'We want goals, we want goals' and with just over half an hour gone, Bobby Charlton obliged with a stunning right-footed drive from 25 yards. BBC commentator Kenneth Wolstenholme described it as 'a beauty'. The hosts were up and running, with Charlton at the centre of most of England's attacks. With 15 minutes remaining Charlton set up Jimmy Greaves, whose low shot was parried by Mexican keeper Ignacio Calderon into the path of Roger Hunt, who scored to secure a 2-0 win.

The final group game, played in front of a packed Wembley crowd, was an incident-packed encounter against a skilful and pacy French team. England's cause was helped by an early injury to France midfielder Robert Herbin that rendered him a passenger for the rest of the game. There were no substitutes in those days, not even for the World Cup. Nobby Stiles, Jimmy Greaves and Jack Charlton combined to set up Roger Hunt for England's opener just before half-time. For this game Ramsey chose Ian Callaghan to play on the wing and it was his cross that was headed home for Hunt's second of the game and third of the competition.

The game would be remembered for two other incidents: Nobby Stiles's controversial crunching tackle on Jacques Simon and a late injury to Jimmy Greaves. The combative tackling of Manchester United's Stiles courted controversy many times in his long career. On this occasion large parts of the public and media thought that not only should Stiles have been sent off, but he should take no further part in the tournament. Ramsey thought otherwise and defended Stiles doggedly. Ramsey was once asked how much the short, gap-toothed, short-sighted and skinny Stiles weighed. 'I would say about 10 stones, but more like 10 tons when he tackles.'

Somewhat surprisingly, Stiles had only made his England debut in April 1965 – against Scotland at Wembley – and his selection surprised many people, including skipper Bobby Moore. But when England were getting battered during the 2-2 draw, Stiles was everywhere, encouraging and pleading for more commitment from his colleagues. His attitude, performance and confidence changed Moore's mind: 'I kept looking at this little fellow and thinking if he could do it, so could the rest of us. After that there was no doubt in my mind he would be included in the World Cup squad and probably the team.'

Perhaps more significant was the injury to Greaves, received when a raking challenge from Joseph Bonnel left the talismanic Tottenham forward needing several stitches in his shin. It meant England would lose their leading goalscorer for the quarter-final encounter with Argentina. Not only that, but Ramsey changed the team's style of play by foregoing wingers and opting for a more flexible 4-3-3 formation with full-backs Fulham's George Cohen and Ramon Wilson from Everton overlapping at every opportunity. He also brought in two of Bobby Moore's team-mates, Martin Peters and Geoff Hurst.

Argentina and Brazil were two of the favourites to triumph in 1966. But both, together with Uruguay, believed they were on the wrong end of a conspiracy led by the hosts. They did have a case, up to a point. Both Argentina and Brazil discovered their respective training grounds had no goals and there were reports of local taxi drivers taking hours to ferry the teams just a few miles for social engagements. The Argentinian squad were also bemused when they were booked into Welwyn Garden City's Homestead Court Hotel instead of a London establishment they had requested. On the pitch, the Brazilian team were butchered by Bulgaria in their opening group game, with Pelé in particular singled out for some really tough treatment. He was kicked so many times that he missed the next game against Hungary, and was made a virtual spectator in their final game against Portugal after João Morais had fouled him and then repeated the treatment as the Brazilian was struggling to his feet. Morais was not cautioned. On his early return to Brazil, Pelé said: 'The games had been a revelation to me in their unsportsmanlike conduct and weak refereeing.'

Argentina finished second in a tough Group Two that also contained group winners West Germany, Spain and Switzerland. But their claims that they were hard done by in their quarter-final tie against England are unfounded. I remember the game well and they were more interested in playing up rather than playing football that day. Skipper Antonio Rattin was the worst culprit and fully deserved his red card. No wonder Ramsey didn't allow George Cohen to swap shirts after the game, which was memorably described by Hugh McIlvanney as 'not so much a football match as an international incident'. Here's how the game, known in Argentina somewhat dramatically as 'El Robo del Siglo' (The Robbery of the Century), unfolded:

From the opening whistle the Argentinians' tactics concentrated on disrupting England's play. The game consisted of a catalogue of fouls – some petty, some dangerous. Although England were guilty of more first-half fouls, the opposition also spent a great deal of time haranguing Rudolf Kreitlein, the diminutive German referee. Orchestrating events was Argentina's skipper,

Antonio Rattin. On the rare occasions that any football was played during the opening half an hour, Argentina showed that they were a more than useful side, forcing Gordon Banks into several fine saves.

Everything changed in the 35th minute when Rattin, who had been constantly needling Kreitlein and had already committed a bad foul on Bobby Charlton, protested against a decision to give England a free kick after Perfumo had fouled Roger Hunt. Another argument ensued and Kreitlein sent Rattin off. In a scene that now looks highly comical, Rattin, at 6ft 3in tall, looked down at Kreitlein, who was a good foot shorter, in disbelief. For almost eight minutes he refused to leave the pitch and, when his coach Juan Carlos Lorenzo signalled to the team to leave the pitch, Rattin, ironically, was the only member of the team on the field. He eventually trudged slowly off, escorted by the police. He still had time to sit on the red carpet, reserved for the Queen, and crumple an England pennant.

England's winning goal came in the 78th minute when Ray Wilson found Martin Peters on the left flank and his left-footed cross to the near post was met by Geoff Hurst, whose glancing header beat goalkeeper Antonio Roma. Almost inevitably the Argentinians claimed Hurst was offside. His finely timed run left him a good two yards onside. At the final whistle England's rivals continued arguing with the referee, who had his shirt ripped. Alf Ramsey famously tried to prevent George Cohen swapping shirts and later described the opposition as 'animals'.

Another quarter-final match saw two World Cup debutants, Portugal and North Korea, face each other. North Korea were the surprise package of the tournament, having beaten the mighty Italy in their final group game to qualify for the last eight. 'The Azzurri' were under great pressure going into this competition, having underperformed four years previously in Chile. Indeed, that 1962 group game against the hosts – which became known as 'The Battle of Santiago' – was a brutal encounter with two dismissals and many punches thrown, and police intervention was needed on four separate occasions. For the record, Chile won 2-0.

David Coleman brilliantly introduced the highlights thus: 'The game you are about to see is the most stupid, appalling, disgusting and disgraceful exhibition of football in the history of the game. This is the first time these countries have met; we hope it will be the last. The national motto of Chile reads, "By Reason or By Force". Today, the Chileans weren't prepared to be reasonable, the Italians only used force, and the result was a disaster for the World Cup.'

The fire had been well stoked before the game started, with two Italian journalists – Antonio Ghirelli and Corrado Pizzinelli – reporting that Santiago was: 'a backwater dump, where the phones don't work, taxis are as rare as faithful husbands, a cable to Europe costs an arm and a leg. Its population is prone to malnutrition, illiteracy, alcoholism and poverty … the country and its people are proudly miserable and backwards.' Chilean newspapers retorted, describing Italians as fascists, mafiosos, oversexed and drug addicts. The last insult was reference to some Inter Milan players that had recently been involved in a doping scandal.

In short, the game had tarnished both nations, but Italy didn't need any more controversy. In fact the 1966 group game between the two sides passed without any violence, with Italy this time winning 2-0. The game against North Korea at Ayresome Park, Middlesbrough, on 19 July was to have a different outcome.

In the build-up to the game, Italian skipper Giacomo Bulgarelli had been doubtful with a knee injury, but manager Edmondo Fabbri gambled on his fitness and included him in the starting XI. But it backfired when Bulgarelli attempted a challenge on Pak Seung-zin and aggravated the injury. With no substitutes, Italy were a man down. It was to get worse just before the interval when Pak Doo-ik let a headed pass from Yong-Won Ha run across his body to drill a low half-volley past Enrico Albertosi and into the corner of the net. It was typical of the North Korean's football style; economic, speedily executed and with minimum fuss – the 1-0 win sealed their place in the quarter-final against Portugal. It looked like the 1,000/1 outsiders were going to provide another upset when they went 3-0 up, but four goals from Eusébio and one from José Torres resulted in a 5-3 win and a semi-final against England. The other two games in the quarter-finals saw West Germany beat Uruguay and the Soviet Union triumph over Hungary.

England v Portugal

Scottish football supporters refer to their country's 3-2 victory over England at Wembley on 15 April 1967 as 'Baxter's game' after Scottish wing-half Jim Baxter put in an inspired performance against the Auld Enemy. By the same token, England's semi-final against Portugal should be known as 'Charlton's game'.

After the spiteful and nasty encounter with Argentina, England's semi-final with Portugal was a breath of fresh air – full of entertaining, attacking football played at a high tempo by two sides who respected each other. It was billed as a showdown between England's Bobby Charlton and Portugal's Eusébio, and the two players didn't disappoint. But it was Charlton and England that came out on top.

Bobby Charlton was superb and, apart from scoring both England goals, he was at the heart of nearly all England's attacks in an entertaining, open and sporting encounter. He seemed to glide elegantly over the Wembley turf, always in control, always looking to go forward with either a trademark mazy run or with one of his raking long balls into the path of Hunt, Hurst or Peters. His first goal came after 30 minutes when he followed up a shot from Roger Hunt that had rebounded off goalkeeper Pereira's legs, calmly slotting it home with his right foot. In the 79th minute George Cohen's clever pass found Geoff Hurst who laid it back to Charlton to thunder a shot into the far corner from the edge of the penalty area.

This was possibly Charlton's best-ever game for his country, but it was also an almost perfect team performance, with all the England players intent on pressing the skilful Portuguese players, giving them little or no time on the ball. In the second half, a Portuguese TV commentator mentioned that Nobby Stiles was always within three metres of Eusébio. In the 'engine room' of England's midfield, Stiles did an admirable job shadowing the Mozambique-born striker and, apart from a couple of rash tackles, competed fairly. He was ably assisted by his hard-working sidekick, Alan Ball, with his defensive team-mates helping out when needed.

Eusébio typified Portugal's sporting attitude when, having converted a penalty given for Jack Charlton's handball with only a few minutes remaining, he still found time to give

Gordon Banks an affectionate smile and pat on the head before running back to the centre circle. England held out for a 2-1 win and Eusébio left the pitch in tears.

The Russian Revolutionary

The other semi-final featured two of the competition's fancied teams, West Germany and the Soviet Union. The game, which took place at Goodison Park, also ended 2-1 in the Germans' favour. It was to be the last time English football fans would be able to see the legendary Soviet Union goalkeeper, Lev Yashin, play in this country. In many English improvised schoolboy kickabout games in the 1960s, the lad chosen to play in goal would often assume the name of the legendary Yashin. It wasn't only because Yashin was considered at that time to be the best goalkeeper ever; it was also because a goalkeeper assuming the name of Springett, West, Stepney or Bloggs sounded typically English. 'A great save by Yashin!' sounds so much better.

Yashin didn't just sound different and charismatic, he was different and charismatic. He certainly looked the part: 6ft 2in and good-looking with slicked-back black hair, he resembled a Hollywood film star of the Cary Grant era. He adopted what looked like a black goalkeeper's kit (in reality it was very dark blue), and often wore a dark cloth cap. Not surprisingly, he was known as the Black Panther or the Black Spider. Yashin is still the only goalkeeper ever to win the Ballon d'Or, in 1962, and the following year he represented the Rest of the World team that played England to celebrate the centenary of the FA. In 1998 he was chosen as part of the World Team of the 20th Century. The team was as follows: Lev Yashin (Soviet Union); Carlos Alberto (Brazil), Franz

Beckenbauer (West Germany), Bobby Moore (England), Nílton Santos (Brazil); Johan Cruyff (Netherlands), Alfredo Di Stéfano (Argentina/Spain), Michel Platini (France); Garrincha (Brazil), Diego Maradona (Argentina), Pelé (Brazil). That's a top team without doubt, but I'm hoping that the likes of Gordon Banks, Bobby Charlton and Ferenc Puskas would have been on the bench!

In domestic matches it was best not to be awarded a spot kick against Yashin's Moscow Dynamo side as he saved an astonishing 151 penalties during his long career. He also recorded over 270 clean sheets. But it wasn't just his shot-stopping that made Yashin stand out; he revolutionised the goalkeeper's role by communicating with and organising the defenders in front of him. He was not afraid to come off his line and intercept crosses and was one of the first stoppers to adopt a sweeper's style of play by advancing out of his area to tidy things up and starting counter-attacks with his positioning and quick throws.

The Final

England boss Alf Ramsey faced a couple of dilemmas before the final against West Germany took place. The team's backroom staff announced that Jimmy Greaves had recovered from his gashed shin and was available for selection. Ramsey stood firm and stayed true to the age-old rule of not changing a winning team, especially as Geoff Hurst had been performing so well. Greaves was understandably upset and in 1986 said: 'I was one of the few people who believed we would win it and what I never ever thought was we would win it without me being in the side.' Greaves wasn't being arrogant but honest. At 26, he was at his peak, one of the most established and talented players in the side and, most importantly, he was a prolific and pacy goalscorer; in theory the ideal man to latch on to Bobby Charlton's through balls. But Ramsey – born in Dagenham, like Greaves – believed Hurst's ability to hold the ball up and give that extra little bit of time for Hunt, Peters and the midfield to get forward suited his game plan better, and so it proved. The other problem was a clash of kit. Both teams played in white shirts, so it was agreed the fairest solution was to toss a coin. The coin was tossed and West Germany won. So on 30 July, in light rain, Bobby Moore led England out on to the wet Wembley pitch wearing red shirts, white shorts and red socks, with German skipper Uwe Seeler and his team sporting white shirts, black shorts and white socks.

England lined up as follows: Gordon Banks; George Cohen, Jack Charlton, Bobby Moore, Ramon Wilson; Alan Ball, Nobby Stiles, Bobby Charlton; Roger Hunt, Geoff Hurst and Martin Peters.

West Germany: Hans Tilkowski; Horst-Dieter Höttges, Willi Schulz, Karl-Heinz Schnellinger; Franz Beckenbauer, Wolfgang Weber, Wolfgang Overath, Helmut Haller; Uwe Seeler, Sigfried Held and Lothar Emmerich.

Interestingly, neither side seemed to be suffering from nerves, with both teams on the front foot from the first minute. England should have been the more confident team as they had never been beaten by their opponents. But, even with Nobby Stiles and Martin Peters looking impressive for England, West Germany started the game the better side, but not before Geoff Hurst made an immediate impact by clattering into German goalkeeper Hans Tilkowski. It was West Germany who opened the scoring in the 12th minute when Held's hopeful cross was met by Ray Wilson's weak header, which fell straight to Haller who scored from 12 yards out.

Six minutes later Bobby Moore was fouled by Wolfgang Overath midway in the opposition's half and his quick free kick found the unmarked Geoff Hurst who headed home from six yards out. The goal rejuvenated not only the England team but also their supporters, and the atmosphere changed from tension to anticipation. Some forgetful English fans immediately started singing 'when the whites go marching in' before realising they were chanting for the opposition!

The game then became a bit scrappy, with referee Gottfried Dienst becoming the busiest man on the pitch, blowing his whistle every few minutes, mainly penalising England for a handful of dubious fouls. Significantly, Alan Ball – apart from Franz Beckenbauer, the youngest player on the pitch – started to exert his influence on the game, his running from deep on a heavy, energy-sapping pitch causing problems for the Germans. Interestingly, Beckenbauer man-marked Bobby Charlton throughout the match, resulting in a situation where they cancelled each other out (the Germans went on to repeat this ploy in the 1970 World Cup quarter-final in Mexico). An even first half ended 1-1 …

Ball carried on where he left off, becoming more of a threat in attack. It was his one-two with Roger Hunt that resulted in a near-post shot forcing Tilkowski into conceding the corner from which England's second goal came. Ball took it and Hurst's shot cannoned off the unfortunate Höttges and fell invitingly to Peters eight yards out. His half-volley found the back of the net. England were ahead with 12 minutes remaining. The Germans were on the front foot and the pressure began to tell on England. The signs weren't good when Nobby Stiles attempted to make an overhead clearance on the edge of his own penalty area, only for him to catch it on the edge of his toe, sending it trickling all of two yards to a grateful and relieved Bobby Moore. Not quite sure why Nobby tried this elaborate trick? Perhaps in the heat of the moment he thought he was his Manchester United team-mate, Denis Law.

They seemed to have done enough until in the last minute Jack Charlton climbed all over Seeler and conceded a free kick 30 yards out. Emmerich blasted it through the English wall and, after a furious skirmish in the six-yard box, Weber scored from close range to break English hearts. There was barely time to restart before Dienst blew his whistle to signal 30 minutes of extra time. Both teams slumped to the ground, only for Alf Ramsey to order his team back on to their feet with the famous words: 'You've beaten them once, now beat them again!'

Alan Ball, with his red socks rolled down, started extra time as he meant to go on and within a minute had made a lung-bursting run from halfway to the edge of the Germans' penalty area, unleashing a dipping drive that Tilkowski tipped over. Shortly after this, Schnellinger pulled up with cramp as the pitch and the pace of the game began to take their toll. Still the action swung from end to end, with England looking slightly the stronger as the game opened up. Hurst once more clattered into Tilkowski after the latter had gathered a fine left-footed cross from an unlikely source – Jack Charlton, who had made an overlap and made himself available to receive a pass from brother Bobby. Bobby then pinged a snap-shot on to Tilkowski's post, the ball rebounding into the goalkeeper's face and then to safety. Then in the 101st minute came the defining moment of the match. Nobby Stiles found Alan Ball in space on the right and his short cross found Geoff Hurst. He controlled the ball, turned and shot against the underside of the bar, and it came down, seemingly over the goal line. Certainly Roger Hunt thought so, raising his hand immediately to salute a goal. Then confusion reigned for several seconds.

Was it a goal? Fifty-four years after the game, that is the question that is always asked. Ultimately, the fact that the officials – referee Gottfried Dienst from Switzerland (always a neutral country!) and, more importantly, Russian linesman Tofiq Bahramov – thought Geoff Hurst's shot had rebounded from the underside of the bar and crossed the line should be enough proof. Brian Moore, commentating for BBC radio, certainly thought it was a goal, saying to his co-commentator: 'I thought that hit the bar and went in, Maurice Edelston.' The nearest player to the incident was England's Roger Hunt and it has often been said that his instinctive reaction of raising his hand in celebration and turning away in triumph, rather than following up and putting the ball in the net, indicates he definitely thought it was over the line.

However, I am writing this the morning after Premier League football resumed after more than three months' inactivity due to the coronavirus pandemic. In the first match played, Sheffield United had a perfectly good goal disallowed in their game against Aston Villa at Villa Park. Shortly before half-time, Villa's goalkeeper Ørjan Nyland carried the ball a foot behind his goal line from Oliver Norwood's free kick. Despite having seven VAR (Video Assistant Referee) Hawk-Eye cameras pointed at the goal, all were obscured by either the goalkeeper, a defender or the goalpost. Referee Michael Oliver and his assistants couldn't see this, but several press cameras show the ball well over the line. If supposedly infallible equipment can't spot an obvious goal, the game has not moved on much since 1966. The record books will simply say Aston Villa 0, Sheffield United 0, just as they say England 4, West Germany 2.

The fourth and final goal came in the last seconds when Bobby Moore, as cool as a cucumber, found enough time and tranquillity in his own penalty area to advance ten yards, look up and strike a perfect 50-yard ball into Geoff Hurst's path. Hurst duly despatched it, accompanied by commentator Kenneth Wolstenholme's immortal line: 'Some people are on the pitch, they think it's all over, it is now.' There's another quote from Jack Charlton, who was standing next to Bobby Moore moments before he made that pass to Hurst: 'I was panicking and screaming at him to just get rid of it. I couldn't believe he was so calm. It was then I realised Bobby Moore played a different game to me.'

Seconds later the final whistle sounded and the whole of the England bench rose to salute an historic victory. All of the bench, apart from one man. Alf Ramsey remained sedate and seated, turning to his assistant Harold Shepherdson and saying: 'Sit down, Shepherdson.'

Yes, hat-trick hero Hurst deserved the headlines but, with his endless running, I believe Alan Ball was England's real hero on the pitch that day. But let's not forget the quiet man behind the scenes who masterminded the whole fantastic journey – Alf Ramsey. And also, for that matter, the other 11 players who made up the 22-man squad. They were: Peter Bonetti, Chelsea; Ron Springett, Sheffield Wednesday; Jimmy

Armfield, Blackpool; Gerry Byrne, Liverpool; Ron Flowers, Wolverhampton Wanderers; Norman Hunter, Leeds United; Ian Callaghan, Liverpool; Terry Paine, Southampton; John Connelly, Manchester United; George Eastham, Arsenal; and Jimmy Greaves, Tottenham Hotspur.

Of those, Jimmy Armfield was among the first to congratulate Ramsey: 'Alf was never the most demonstrative person I've ever seen. You could never say he was infectious, but I liked his strength of silence.' Nobby Stiles, whom Ramsey backed after the France game and remembered for his joyous jig in the post-match celebrations, says: 'Because he was loyal to you, you'd run through brick walls for him. And it wasn't just the players. Everyone concerned with England was doing it for Alf.' The final word on Ramsey goes to Geoff Hurst: 'We had some tremendous individual players and we all had one thing in common – Sir Alf Ramsey. It's easy to spot players who have ability. What's not so straightforward is realising which personalities will combine well to form a strong team. That was Alf's strength.'

All the great British football managers have similar attributes to Ramsey – Robson, Mercer, Clough, Ferguson, Busby, Paisley, Stein and Graham Taylor too. One thing that set Ramsey apart was his utter devotion to his players, coupled with an often frosty relationship with the media, which made him unique. It is doubtful if he could have managed in these modern times. He surely wouldn't have liked the 24/7 media attention and constant need for sound bites. And in a way, who can blame him? You have to admire a man who, when asked by a TV presenter for his opinion after a particularly impressive England performance, replied deadpan: 'You could say I was not displeased.'

CHAPTER 5

Big School and Mr College

MY SECONDARY education began at Francis Combe Comprehensive in September 1966. Although the first comprehensives were established after the Second World War, it wasn't until 1966 that they became popular. This followed a policy decision in 1965 by Anthony Crosland, the then Secretary of State for Education and Science in Harold Wilson's Labour government.

It was all a bit of a shock to my system as my schooling had been easy-going up to this point. I was used to a sedate stroll of no more than 20 yards across the road to primary school where there were probably no more than 150 pupils. Now I had to catch a bus from the end of my road and then walk a mile down Horseshoe Lane in Garston, in all a 40-minute trip in the morning and slightly longer in the afternoon. The longer journey was because the return bus stop in Bricket Wood was a further 400 yards up the dual carriageway, meaning I had a much longer walk back home. The school seemed massive too, both in terms of the size of the place and in the number of children there, all rushing around like demented ants. They all seemed to know where they were going, but my dire sense of direction combined with my new surroundings meant that it took me ages to find my way around. I was used to having just one class in primary school and the teachers came to me. Now I had to get to them! To begin with it was pretty tricky and took some getting used to.

The teachers were different too; not exactly unfriendly, but they didn't look as if they would be giving you much encouragement, and cuddles looked even more unlikely. My form teacher, Mr Moffatt, was a Scotsman who specialised in English and Sarcasm. Very early on he told the class that we should all read the English dictionary from start to finish. We thought he was barmy and ignored his advice. Years later, when I was in my thirties, I realised he was right and that it was and is a great idea. This reminds me of Mark Twain's assessment of his father: 'When I was a boy of 14, my father was so ignorant I could hardly stand to have the old man around. But when I got to be 21, I was astonished at how much he had learned in seven years.'

The other English teacher was a mild-mannered man, Mr Fitzpatrick, who was responsible for encouraging my love of books. *Catch 22*, *Cider with Rosie*, passages of E.M. Forster, Steinbeck, Shakespeare, Gerald Durrell, Somerset Maugham and especially Dylan Thomas's *Under Milk Wood* were all consumed with relish. C.P. Snow and Chaucer were harder to enjoy, but I read them anyway. Being introduced to the work of Dylan Thomas was an eye-opener. The way he used and played with words was new to me and had a profound effect not only on how I read but on how I wrote too. It was thanks to Thomas, Mr Fitzpatrick and also Liverpool-born poet

Roger McGough that I started dabbling in poetry when I was in my teens. When I was starting to take an interest in one or two girls at school, the teenage torment I experienced was soothed by writing poetry. I enjoyed it a great deal and even joined a poetry group in St Albans, Ver Poets, where I read a couple of my pieces on my first and only visit. Although they were initially well received by the bunch of elderly, serious and rather dull people put before me, they spent the next five minutes or so dissecting and criticising my work. I don't think they were Dylan Thomas, Roger McGough or Ivor Cutler fans, probably never heard of them. Suffice to say, I didn't return. Perhaps I was being immature and oversensitive but, all these years later, I believe I would have done exactly the same thing now.

I countered the more mundane aspects of my new school life by concentrating on getting myself into the school football team. A few of my fellow pupils from Mount Pleasant Lane accompanied me to my new school, including Paul Hunt and Keith Slaney, and we all set about achieving our goal.

The PE master and football manager was Mike Dixon, a super-fit young teacher who was a superb long-distance runner and athlete, but knew little about football. We all chuckled when, in an early training session, he told us we would be practising a new drill called 'the wall pass'. But by mixing cross-country running with circuit training we quickly got fit.

Mike Dixon was certainly as fit as a fiddle, but he was found wanting when he confronted a rowdy fifth former in the playground during the first week of school. A scuffle ensued and Dixon asked the boy for his name. 'Shitface!' was the lout's reply. Just as the teacher looked like coming out second best, he was rescued by the slightly effeminate and bulky music teacher, Mr Davies, who lifted the lout by the back of his neck and hoisted him off to the headmaster's study.

Appearances can be deceptive and we soon learnt that the brown-corduroy-jacketed, blond-haired Mr Davies was tougher than he looked. For instance, if you were talking during a lesson his party piece was to sneak up behind you and hit you on the back of the head with a rubber-headed glockenspiel hammer. Take my word for it, the pain was excruciating! Violence of some sort was part of a teacher's armoury back then, and rumour had it that our former GB weightlifter and history teacher, Mr Newton, once tried out a pupil's crossbow that had just been built during metalwork. He aimed it at the classroom door and the bolt went straight through before becoming embedded in another class's door across the corridor. Luckily no one was passing by at the time or Mr Newton would have been serving time.

Our school football team had some useful players. Captain was Robert Peck, a happy, communicative centre-half, with Dave 'Drag-Back' Holt up front along with outside-right Lance Dudley. Lance was primarily an athlete, like Mr Dixon, and he was very quick with a tremendous shot. Graham Goss was our dependable goalkeeper. But star of the team was centre-forward Ronald Brimson, who scored goals for fun. I remained at right-back and we won far more games than we lost. In fact, we were league champions for the first two years.

I was about eight when I was told that, like my brother, I needed to wear glasses. So I was promptly carted off to see Mr Appel. He was the optician in Watford who Laurie had been visiting for the past few years. Karl Appel was a bald, softly-spoken Austrian who looked a little like Donald Pleasence's character, Blythe 'The Forger', in *The Great Escape* and, because of this, appeared to me quite scary. Laurie's impression of him, delivered a day or two prior to my first eye test, didn't fill me with much confidence either. My brother would adopt a quiet German-tinged accent similar to a Second World War SS officer and proceeded to prepare me for what I should expect at my first examination. Pacing around the front room, he would say in a whisper: 'Ant now, Paul, I vood like you to tell me vot eye is my finger int front of now. Is it za left eye or za rright eye? Relax, zare ist nothink to vorry about. Vot is it, za left eye or za rright?' By now I was beginning to panic and wriggle in my seat, perspiration was appearing on my brow. 'Za left eye or za rright eye?' 'Um, I'm not sure but I think it's the right eye ...' In a flash Laurie's Mr Appel would explode into a screaming madman: 'It is not za right eye! It is za left eye, za left eye, you stupid idiot!' Yes, Stanley Kubrick's *Dr Strangelove* has a lot to answer for!

Luckily, it turned out Laurie had been exaggerating more than somewhat and the eye examination was peacefully conducted without any hint of violence or torture. My new glasses duly arrived and by the time I was 13 I needed them to play football. This was not a problem until, during a freezing-cold match at Queen's School in Watford, the ball hit me on my forehead and forced the metal frame to sink into my right eye and surrounding socket. Not only did it hurt, but it also left me with a black eye Henry Cooper would have been proud of. Dad, already critical of Mr Appel's expensive glasses, decided I should under no circumstances wear glasses for football again. So for the next few years I had to hang up my boots until contact lenses became a realistic and affordable option.

Mr Dixon did approach me a few months after my eye accident to see if I wanted to start playing football again. I was flattered and was seriously considering it until he added: 'For the third team.' Pride got the better of me and I politely declined.

At around this time my football education was helped a great deal by the kindness and thoughtfulness of two elderly ladies. Firstly, my dad's older sister, Auntie Joan, who lived in Whetstone, north London, started to send me copies of *Charles Buchan's Football Monthly*. As soon as the rolled-up brown-paper-wrapped parcel, addressed to Master Paul Bishop, fell through our letterbox, I felt a thrill of expectation and excitement. After all, what young boy wouldn't be excited to be singled out like this? I had been told by my mum that the magazines had originally been read by my cousin Roger, and Joan had recycled them in my direction. Mum later admitted that this was not true and that Joan bought and mailed them just for me.

Charles Buchan was a former Sunderland and Arsenal centre-forward turned journalist and BBC commentator. He launched and edited the magazine that bears his name in 1951 and it was published until 1974.

The other lady was a neighbour and friend of my mum's, Mrs Lane. She lived three doors down the road, drove a Ford Cortina like my dad and, unlike Dad, was an avid Watford fan. I expect my parents asked her if she wouldn't mind taking me with her to and from the weekend home fixtures. She must have agreed as a few weeks later I was travelling with her and her accomplice, a fellow Bricket Wood pensioner, Mr College. Both were season-ticket holders and sat in the Shrodells Stand so, once she had parked up close to the ground, I would walk up to the stadium on my own and meet a few of my school friends outside the Vicarage Road end. Once inside, we would walk round to the tea stall next door to the main stand. It was situated in a small concrete area that must have been used by the players for shooting practice as there was a very smart RAF-style target painted on the wall.

After our cuppa and chocolate snacks, we would gather midway between the Vicarage Road end and the Shrodells Stand to wait for the pre-game tossing of the coin. This was a ritual undertaken by many schoolchildren as the gate near the halfway line would be opened to let the crowd through if Watford kicked towards the Rookery end. If that was the case, we would hurriedly walk round to take our place in the Rookery enclosure for the first half and then traipse back again for the second half. I, like many other children, preferred the Vicarage Road end as the Rookery steps were so shallow that you would struggle to see your favourite stars like Stewart Scullion, Terry Garbett and Keith 'Steady' Eddy …

This was the 1966/67 season, when Watford were stuck in mid-table mediocrity in the Third Division and home attendances averaged around the 7,000 mark. Whatever the result and whatever the attendance, the drive back with Mrs Lane and Mr College would usually consist of Mrs Lane saying: 'Mind you, I did think the referee was on their side.' Mr College didn't say much, but it was far from a silent trip as Mr College suffered from wind that, when he was in full flow, sounded like a trombone blast from George Chisholm on the BBC's Saturday night *Black and White Minstrel Show.*

There were considerably more than 7,000 for the visit of Liverpool in the third round of the FA Cup on 28 January 1967; approximately 26,000 more! And I was one of them, at a game I always call 'Shoegate'. For some reason I didn't get my usual lift with Mrs Lane, instead travelling to the game on the 321 bus. I positioned myself in the heart of the Vicarage Road end, standing in a brand-new pair of black slip-on shoes. The game ended in a 0-0 stalemate and I left, along with everyone else. Climbing up the steps to the exit was tricky, but a doddle compared to being confronted by a combination of heavy rain and a mass of spectators that filled Vicarage Road. I couldn't move. Not a single step. However, I was levitated and transported no more than six inches off the ground about 300 yards up the road by a huge crowd of adults. At some point I was lowered a few inches so that the tip of my left foot was dragging along the pavement. I suddenly felt the bloody shoe slip off and, when the crowd started to thin out, I trudged the rest of the way to the bus stop with only one shoe and a soaking sock. When I got home Mum told me off and asked why I didn't go back for the shoe. I told her it was impossible as there were too many people behind me. I suppose I could have walked back a bit later to reclaim it, but I was a bit traumatised by my unusual journey back to the bus stop.

I continued to be a 'fair-weather supporter' for the rest of that season; my parents would limit me to games played when the weather was dry and not too cold. I don't believe they were being overprotective. I am now a parent of an 11-year-old son, as well as a teenage daughter, and would not allow my son to travel to home games alone. In a year or so, when Laurie was not at school on a Saturday morning, or when a midweek home game was on during half-term, we would travel together via bus to the Watford Junction stop and join the throng of supporters coming off the trains to walk to the ground from there.

Two presents I remember receiving for Christmas in 1966 were a Beatle Wig and the table-top football game, Subbuteo. Although I enjoyed wearing the wig for a while, it's fair to say that it always looked better on Grandad Bishop, who wore it when we visited Auntie Joan's house for the annual Boxing Day family gathering, which for us was the high point of seasonal festivities.

It really was a magical time for me, and not just because I received the bulk of my gifts there – although this obviously helped! Joan always put an awful lot of effort into this event, making piles of sandwiches, snacks and cakes. There was also a fair amount of beer, wine and spirits for the grown-ups. I had my first taste of alcohol there when I was treated to a glass of mead – a mix of honey, water, fruits, spices and hops. It was lovely, but probably watered down by Joan's husband, Gerry, who was notoriously mean. Dad said 'he had short arms and long pockets'. Dad also suspected Gerry of watering down the grown-ups' drinks as well, but I don't think this was ever proved.

These festive get-togethers attracted most of my dad's side of the family including, on one or two occasions, my Uncle Jack, whom Dad had christened the 'black sheep' of the family. Dad also told me that Jack had never fully forgiven him for taunting him when they were children by mercilessly making fun of his stutter. Dad said that if Jack had caught him he would have murdered him. Luckily, Dad was quick on his feet. Jack worked as a journalist at the *Daily Express* as a copy-taker. He also lived on his own in a flat in Broad Court, Covent Garden, and was a regular in the nearby Brahms and Liszt wine bar; he even had his own table near to the entrance. He also seemed to have an on-off relationship with his partner, 'Auntie Nina'. Nina was a dark-haired Spanish-looking lady whose jet-black hair was parted in the middle. She wore lots of make-up and large hooped earrings. I was always aware that the grown-ups would be talking from time to time about Jack and what he had been getting up to.

He was a bit of a hero to me and, several years later, when I was in my early twenties and working in London, I arranged to meet him for a drink in Brahms and Liszt. From the moment I walked through the door and met Jack, it was obvious the rendezvous was far more important for me. He wasn't rude (he immediately bought me a glass of wine), but as this was the first time I'd ever stepped into a wine bar, I was out of my depth. I was used to pubs or, to be precise, two pubs – The Fox and Hounds in Bricket Wood, where I went with Dad, and The Lamb in Lamb's Conduit Street, which was 200 yards from where I worked. We sat chatting about journalism for about half an hour or so and I offered to buy him a glass of red wine. He declined, saying he had to leave and meet some friends. We left and I never saw him again, although I did inherit his typewriter after he died, alone in his flat, a few years later. Jack was a one-off and I was a bit too young and naive to fully understand him. I was still just a boy and, in a perfect world, it would have been better if I had met him when I was a bit older. But life's not like that, and anyway, his attitude would have been exactly the same. He was part Terry-Thomas, part Graham Greene and I loved him. I have since met and worked with a lot of journalists and many have a slightly jaundiced and ironic view of their work and their life. The trouble was, I didn't know that then.

The day after my brief meeting with Jack, Dad enquired how it went? 'Short and not so sweet,' I replied. After I explained more fully what had happened, my dad laughed and told me not to worry, as Jack hadn't even managed to attend his wedding! Instead he sent a telegram that read: 'I'm highly delighted, we're all highly delighted, (signed) Haile Selassie.'

Jack was a huge influence and one of the main reasons I became a writer. Here's a short poem of his that sums up his whimsical style:

If you run in grooves along the highway,
And travel down the middle just for fun,
Yours is the street and everything that's in it,
And what is more you'll be a tram my son.

The following football season, a few of my friends – who were not Watford fans – had become fed up with watching a Third Division side week in and week out and decided to watch Chelsea instead. I went with them to a few games to keep them company. To be fair, Chelsea were one of the top teams at this time, mixing the flair of John Hollins, Charlie Cooke and Alan Hudson with the force of Ron 'Chopper' Harris, Eddie McCreadie and David Webb. To add to the excitement, the trip to Stamford Bridge was great fun as, apart from a visit to the West End with my Auntie Olive to see The Beatles' film *Help* a year or so before, London was new to me. I don't remember being overawed by the size of the crowd and I was fairly relaxed watching a game where the result was not important, unlike my trips to Vicarage Road, where the nervous jitters started an hour or so before kick-off. We stood on the terraces opposite The Shed, not daring to go anywhere near it as it was full of violent-looking skinheads who could probably spot a mild-mannered Hertfordshire accent a mile away. I didn't know it at the time, but I was inadvertently doing a spying job on Chelsea as we were to play them in an FA Cup semi-final a couple of years later.

But back to Subbuteo. I had always assumed it was an Italian game, and not, as it turns out, invented by Peter Adolph from Tunbridge Wells. This makes me feel a little silly as I can remember commentating on the games in an exaggerated Italian accent, rather like the Italian officer in *'Allo 'Allo*. Whatta mistakah to makeaa!

I was given a basic version of the game consisting of two teams, goals, pitch and an oversized football, which in scale was almost as tall as the players. It looked ridiculous and I soon replaced it with the smaller, more realistic ball, the first of many accessories I would buy. One of the teams had blue shirts, white shorts and socks. That was Everton. The other had red shirts, with white shorts and socks, and that was Manchester United. I soon added a light blue and white team – Manchester City – and a white and dark blue team – Tottenham Hotspur. Matches were never played on a table, but on the carpet in the lounge. This was because the kitchen table had a hard black and white resin top and was immediately deemed unsuitable by myself and also Mum.

The lounge floor was perfect, the only drawback being when Candy the family cat sauntered in and started pawing players, pitch, ball and goals in a feline frenzy. I would then assume the Italian commentator routine, introducing elements of horror films like *King Kong* or the *Creature from the Black Lagoon*: 'And anow we have something of a surprise a 'ere in Napoli where a the 'ome team are being attacked by a giant pussy cat bya the name of Candy! She's agoing crazy and itta look as though Betalucci is in trouble on the left winga with a badda knocka.' We tried to banish Candy from the stadium by shutting the door, but eventually she would creep through a window or find a way of entering the room to interrupt the game again, prompting the Italian commentator to carry on where he had left off.

Another downside of playing on the carpet floor was that the players, usually myself or Laurie, would accidentally kneel on one of the plastic players, causing a serious injury. Dad was at this time a big fan of a glue called Araldite, having switched from Bostik a few years previously. Araldite is a two-part epoxy adhesive that requires the user to mix a resin with a hardener. I soon became an expert on the mixing part, but the problems started when I tried to apply a small part on the plastic players' ankles at the base. You needed the patience and dexterity of an expert safe-cracker, neither of which I possessed. As a result, the injured players, after gluing, would be placed on top of the boiler in the kitchen to dry. On a bad day there would be as many as four or five sad-looking plastic players sitting side by side on the boiler, with more glue than legs.

I tried several times to buy a Watford set of players, but at that time a yellow and black team wasn't available. No problem. I improvised by taking the Tottenham team and, with some yellow and black paint and a tiny old brush from an Airfix set, Spurs soon turned into Watford. They looked great and I was especially pleased with how left-back Johnny Williams turned out. I very carefully managed to paint on a replica of his Mexican-style droopy moustache that he had recently been sporting. Watford could now compete against Everton and Manchester City who, in 1967/68, were two of the most successful and entertaining clubs in the country. Under the managerial team of Joe Mercer and Malcolm

Allison, Manchester City were Division One champions in 1968 and the team included the veteran skipper Tony Book, Colin Bell, Francis Lee, Neil Young and Mike Summerbee. Harry Catterick's Everton were runners-up in the FA Cup and finished fifth in the league. With Ramon Wilson in defence and a midfield of Howard Kendall, Alan Ball and Colin Harvey, plus Joe Royle and Alex Young in attack, they were a force to be reckoned with. Alex Young was a hero at Goodison Park and the quietly-spoken Scot even had a TV drama, *The Golden Vision,* directed by Ken Loach, based on him.

After a few months I started to visit some school friends' houses to play and discovered I was quite good at the game. I do remember once playing Laurie on a carpet pitch in the kitchen. This was the only time we played there, and I presume the reason was Mum must have been hosting one of her coffee mornings in the lounge. I started the game well and was soon two or three goals up. Good news for me, not so for my brother, who was not only five and a half years older than me, but highly competitive too. I made the usual mistake of winding him up with some light-hearted banter when the next goal went in. In a rage he lifted the pitch from the floor, scattering most of the players under the fridge and, mouthing obscenities under his breath, stormed out to his bedroom. I panicked and quickly gathered all 22 players together to make sure they were all OK and that no Araldite treatment was required. I breathed a sigh of relief on discovering there had been no casualties.

A few years later, a similar thing happened during a summer tennis match at my school courts down the road. It took place during the summer holidays, but the caretaker knew me because Dad and I had played a few games there over the previous month or so. Laurie and I had already had a couple of matches that he had narrowly won. I was improving fast and getting stronger, and I knew I was close to beating him. It was a beautiful summer's day and quite warm when we started playing. The match was fairly even early on, but I started to get ahead and a mix of his frustration and my new-found confidence resulted in a straightforward victory that tasted really sweet. Far from running up to the net and shaking hands, like they did at Wimbledon, Laurie hit all four balls high into the air and into the woods behind the court, before calling me 'an obnoxious prig' and storming off across the field on his way back home. I was left alone to forlornly try and find the balls in the deep undergrowth, feeling pleased yet fearful – pleased to have beaten him and fearful of his temper when I got back home. When I eventually arrived home, I kept well out of his way until normal service was resumed.

At its peak, my devotion to Subbuteo was so great that I decided to invest in the cricket version. As both batting and bowling were extremely difficult to perfect, I doubt if the game was a commercial success. For instance, the batsman would have to hold a small horizontal plastic handle, which was held between forefinger and thumb, to operate the bat. If you think this sounds difficult, wait until you had to bowl! At the rear of the bowling figure was a small triangular metal piece where the ball would go. To project it towards the batsman, you had to flick his head forward like a cartwheel to get the ball somewhere near the wicket. Most of the time the ball either dribbled a couple of inches or was catapulted 20 yards behind the batsman and landed under the sofa. I gave up after about ten minutes and replaced the batsman with an AAA-sized battery and put the bowler back in the box, flicking the ball instead with my index finger. I could now play on my own and, on a good day, replicate a limited-overs version of the game. When the ball hit the battery in the right place, it would either race to the boundary or be 'caught' by one of the fielders, which had a special recess built into the base. For the commentary I would be John Arlott, with comments supplied by Richie Benaud: 'That's a magnificently powerful shot from Ever Ready, and Trueman's not too pleased about it and is giving him the glare. I think he's muttering a few choice words under his breath too.' 'You're right, John, good shot that, it's gone through the confectionery stall and out the other side. Nearly took the top off that gentleman's strawberry sundae too.'

My adaptation of Subbuteo cricket was not the only time my creativity and ingenuity were at work within the sporting-games sector. During my time in the sixth form, I devised an alternative to table tennis. Instead of playing for points, two tea mugs, both almost full of water, were placed at each end of the table. The two players would then attempt to get the ball into the mug. When the ball landed with a plop into the mug it made a really satisfying sound and, despite being a bit messy, caught on quickly. I even came up with a snappy name for the game: 'Getting De Ping-Pong Ball In De Mug Competition.' Soon it was decided we should have a school tournament. I was hooked and won nearly all of the best-of-three games myself and a few friends played. Having invented the game I was naturally the number-one seed and I was drawn, in the first round, to play a 12-year-old first-form girl who had never played before. I soon got my eye in and hit the rim of the mug several times, whilst my opponent, quite understandably, struggled to hit the ball – not surprising really, as she was so little she could hardly see above the edge of the table. I knew it would only be a matter of minutes before I scored the two points necessary to progress to the quarter-finals. Then, from nowhere, the girl scored the first point. The crowd that had gathered to watch this opening match sensed an upset. I was still confident that my opponent had just got lucky and that I would soon wrap up the match. But still I couldn't score and, inevitably, the girl put me out of my misery by scoring soon afterwards. A 2-0 defeat. She was the new favourite until she was knocked out in the next round, never looking like she'd score a point. It was left to fellow sixth-former, Charlie Matcham, to take home the winner's mug. But it was me who felt the biggest mug of all!

My Subbuteo craze lasted about three years and by that time I had acquired a few accessories to add to the basics that were in the original set. These included a set of floodlights, which were a total waste of time. The most memorable and bizarre item was marketed as 'apparatus for keeping the ball in the net', and turned out to be a piece of modified double-sided Sellotape. Years later it was gratifying to learn that I was not alone in my obsession for Subbuteo. Tranmere fans Half Man Half Biscuit's 'All I Want For Christmas Is a Dukla Prague Away Kit' is a humorous nod to the game: 'So he sent his doting mother up the stairs with the stepladder, to get the Subbuteo out of the loft. He had all the accessories required for that big-match atmosphere. The crowd and the dugout and the floodlights too. And you'd always get palmed off with the headless centre-forward and a goalkeeper with no arms.' They obviously didn't have Araldite in Liverpool.

I like the following story, which typifies these Liverpool lads' eccentricity. They had a slot booked on *The Tube*, the prestigious mid-80s Friday evening TV music programme, presented by Jools Holland and Paula Yates. The band turned it down as Tranmere were playing at home that night! Ulster band The Undertones also mention Subbuteo in their hit single 'My Perfect Cousin' when Feargal Sharkey sings: 'He always beats me at Subbuteo, 'cos he flicks to kick and I didn't know.' The sleeve of the record depicts a Subbuteo figure in the colours of the band's local club, Derry City.

As well as *Charles Buchan's Football Monthly,* I used to buy *Shoot*, especially at the start of a new football season when the magazine's free gift was invariably the league ladders. These were cardboard charts with all the 92 league clubs represented by push-out labels with their name in club colours. Whenever a teacher or another adult would question my love of football, I would think of all the subjects the sport helped me with. For instance, seeing all the 92 English and Welsh league clubs, and also many Scottish and non-league teams, represented like this helped me with my spelling and also geography. Over time I have managed to develop the ability to reproduce a map of UK towns and cities in my mind from Alloa to York. League tables aided my maths, as does goal difference. I am sure I was not the only child to be able to do this.

Over the years I have built up a big collection of football-related books. Some, like John Tennant's *Football: The Golden Age,* feature many magnificent vintage black and white photographs of obscure football scenes. A couple that stick in my mind show Jack and Bobby Charlton's mother arriving at Euston station, being greeted by railway staff on her way to Wembley for the World Cup Final. The other shot shows players from Manchester City and Birmingham City with their backs to the camera, waiting in the tunnel at Wembley before the 1956 FA Cup Final. Images like these can easily ignite an interest in photography.

CHAPTER 6

Football on Film and TV

ONE THING all football fans need is a sense of humour, especially if you support one of the less successful clubs. I used to get annoyed when Liverpool supporters phoned in to the *606* show on Radio 5 Live in the late 90s and early 2000s, in the days when Gérard Houllier and Rafa Benitez were in charge. If they hadn't won for a couple of games, they would be moaning and groaning, complaining that a new manager was the answer. These supporters assumed they had the right to win every game, but we all know that this is not possible. To their credit, many fans from the north-west of the country have a tremendous sense of humour, much of it self-deprecating and laced with a fair amount of irony too.

Having a laugh is important on the terraces, in the car, coach or train travelling to and from away games, or in the pub for that pre or post-match pint. Luckily, both Mum and Dad introduced me to a great many comedians and entertainers from an early age. Mum was a huge fan of the wireless, as the radio was known back in those days in the

1960s; it was on constantly and at a good volume so it could be heard throughout the house. One of the first presenters I remember was Jack Jackson, whose *Record Roundup* show was broadcast on the BBC *Light Programme* on Saturday lunchtimes. Jackson was a trumpeter and band leader, born in Barnsley in 1906, and had a unique style for that time, incorporating extracts from various comedy records and pre-recorded tapes. Artists that were often featured included Tony Hancock, The Goons and Steptoe and Son. His style was way ahead of its time and influenced the likes of Kenny Everett, amongst others. Jackson also came up with the BBC's nickname of Auntie.

Another radio show that amused me was the *Billy Cotton Band Show* on Sunday lunchtimes. Cotton – a large, loud Cockney character – was also a band leader and introduced the show with the cry of 'Wakey-Wake-aaaay!' followed by the band's theme tune of 'Somebody Stole My Gal'. The show was also shown on BBC TV on Saturday evenings, with future *Monty Python* stars Michael Palin and Terry Jones writing the jokes. Other shows and personalities I learned to love included Brian Matthew's *Saturday Club* and *Workers' Playtime*, where Peter Sellers, Terry-Thomas, Tony Hancock, Frankie Howerd, Ken Dodd and Morecambe and Wise often featured.

I was also impressed with a hit tune from Scottish folk duo, Robin Hall and Jimmie Macgregor – 'Football Crazy' – that was released in 1959 and was popular in the early 60s, getting loads of play on the radio. It is the earliest known football song and was written in the 1880s by songwriter James Curran, who was born in County Donegal, Ireland, but later moved to Glasgow. The song was originally called 'The

Dooley Fitba' Club' and sung by J.C. M'Donald. I found it both funny and fascinating, mainly because I couldn't understand the lyrics, which go like this:

You all know my big brither Jock
His right name's Johnny Shaw.
Last week he jined a fitba' club
For he's mad about fitba'.
He's got two black eyes already,
An' teeth oot by the root,
Since Jock's face came in contact
Wi another fella's boot.

Chorus

'Cause he's fitba' crazy,
He's fitba' mad.
The fitba' it has ta'en away
The wee bit sense he had.
And it wid take a dozen servants
His claes tae wash and scrub,
Since Jock became a member o'
That terrible fitba' club.
The first game he took part in,
I wis there ma'sel' an' saw,
There were twa half bricks fae goalposts,
An' a tin can for the ba'.
The Prince of Wales wis present,
Wi' lords 'n' ladies grand –
Oor Jock he got an egg box,
An' he made a big grandstand.

Chorus

Oh all the fitba' teams hiv afloat,
He swears they are the prime.

An' you want tae hear him bounce aboot
Their beatin' record time.
They've challenged every ither side
Nane 'ill tak' them up,
Since they beat the Blind Asylum
Fir a leather plated cup.

Chorus

His wife she says she'll leave him,
If he disnae keep
Away frae playin' fitba'.
At night time in his sleep,
He ca's her Pat McGinty,
An' ither names sae droll.
Last night he kicked her oot the bed
An' swore it wis a goal!

See what I mean? And I'm sure it was skivvies instead of servants in the chorus, Jimmy!

Meanwhile Dad would regularly bring home the latest music and comedy records from work. These included *Beyond the Fringe* with Peter Cook, Dudley Moore, Jonathan Miller and Alan Bennett; *At The Drop of a Hat* by Michael Flanders and Donald Swann; 'Charlie Brown' backed with 'Three Cool Cats' by The Coasters; 'Goldiloppers and the Three Bearloders' by Professor Stanley Unwin; 'The Driving Instructor' by Bob Newhart; *Songs for Swinging Sellers* by Peter Sellers; and various Fats Waller, Frank Sinatra and Tony Bennett records.

As well as attending live games during the 1960s, I could also enjoy football on the television; 1968 was a big year for sports shows. It was the year BBC's *Sportsnight with Coleman* (later *Sportsnight*) and ITV's *The Big Match* were launched.

Although the former covered all sports, its presenter, David Coleman, was already an influential and established journalist and presenter, having been the anchorman of BBC1's Saturday afternoon sports programme *Grandstand* since 1958. The fiercely competitive and professional Coleman was respected and admired by his peers, even though his somewhat brusque and confident delivery could be interpreted as arrogant at times, and there were rumours that he wasn't easy to work with.

But fellow journalist Frank Keating described him in his obituary piece for *The Guardian* as having 'an enthusiastic, knowing, taut professional style and a crisp, classless delivery that seemed all-pervading ... the pathfinding master of ceremonies for such long-running regulars as *Grandstand, Sportsnight* and *A Question of Sport*.' He really was BBC's 'Mr Sport', leading their coverage of 16 Olympic Games (summer and winter), five World Cups, numerous cup finals and Grand Nationals and countless athletics events. Keating again: 'He realised that the knack of successful television commentary required both passion and brevity, as well as, for the most important passages, bestowing a significantly precise top and tail to frame the occasion for posterity, as in: "This then, the start of the 200 metres of the 1976 Olympic Games ..." to "Oh, what a run, what a run, truly magnificent!" Rivals were never comfortable with Coleman. In the mid-1960s, when ITV hired Eamonn Andrews to launch its Saturday afternoon *World of Sport* magazine programme to take on *Grandstand*, Coleman dismissively told Andrews: "I'll blow you out of the water!" And mercilessly that's just what he did.'

But I remember Coleman, who was to replace Kenneth Wolstenholme as *Match of the Day* host in 1967, was at his best beside the legendary *Grandstand* teleprinter, unflappably reading the teatime football results. So did Keating: 'Queen of the South one, Airdrie one, means Airdrie move up three places on goal difference, but Queen of the South slip a place because Brechin won today.' Brilliant from both Coleman and Keating! His real passion was best exemplified when he was commentating on his favourite sport – athletics. His emotional coverage of Ann Packer's gold-medal-winning run in the 800 metres in the 1964 Olympic Games in Tokyo is extra special. The BBC were blessed with many truly great sports commentators in the 60s and 70s – like Dan Maskell on tennis, Henry Longhurst on golf, and John Arlott on cricket – and David Coleman deservedly joins that elite group.

Football's first dedicated programme was *Match of the Day*. It was launched on BBC2 on Saturday, 22 August 1964 and the 50-minute slot was devoted to highlights from a single First Division game, in this case between Liverpool and Arsenal. The programme was introduced by Kenneth Wolstenholme, assisted by co-commentator Wally Barnes. This game was exciting, but not particularly pretty, with lots of misplaced passes from both teams, but the last-minute winning goal from Liverpool's Gordon Wallace, created by Ian Callaghan, gave Wolstenholme something to cheer about. He described it somewhat extravagantly to Wally Barnes afterwards: 'Never mind the Match of the Day, but possibly the match of the century!'

A year later, Watford featured on a BBC news programme when Alan Weeks and a camera crew visited the squad in the Lake District, where they were undergoing ten days of pre-season training at a farm in 'Wordsworth country', Loweswater. It was manager Ken Furphy's idea and served not only as an extended training session but as a team-bonding exercise too. Furphy was a local lad and had been there with his previous club, Workington. It was a tough regime, with all the players and staff sleeping in tents when not running and hiking up mountains or swimming and bathing in freezing-cold lakes. Food was cooked by members of the Bushey Scout troop, who had travelled up with the team by coach.

Keeping a close eye on the players was legendary trainer/physio Pat Molloy, whom the camera caught waking the boys up with an impressive display of yodelling. Molloy was as tough as nails and was a forerunner of Tom Walley in many ways. Born in the area of Rossendale, south of Burnley, he had tried his hand as a boxer in a travelling fair, where he took on and beat all-comers, whatever size. He even thought about doing it professionally until a friend died after taking part in one fight too many. He then took on a career in football with Fulham, Cardiff, Queens Park Rangers and Bradford City, amongst others. He moved on to coach Galatasaray in Turkey and then accepted an offer to join Watford.

Cliff Holton, newly arrived for his second spell at the club, has a chat with Alan Weeks, who introduces Holton, saying, 'He is called "The King" by the younger players,' before asking him how he is coping with the trip. 'It's a new experience for me, but I think it's the type of training that will breed good team spirit. It's a situation where you all muck in together and make the best of it. All the lads here are doing that and we're enjoying it and have settled in. When we first arrived we looked around and said, "What have we let ourselves in for?" and thought that bathing in the brook was ridiculous, but we quite enjoy it.'

Ken Furphy is also interviewed by Weeks, telling him that he hoped the trip would result in the team being one of the fittest in the country. The five-minute film finishes with the team singing enthusiastically to The Kingston Trio's 'My Ramblin' Boy' around the campfire.

There were only three television channels available in 1968 – BBC1, ITV and BBC2, which was launched in April 1964. BBC2's remit was to broadcast on less mainstream and more ambitious arts-based programmes, so it was ironic that the channel was launched with a children's show called *Play School.* However, when David Attenborough took over as controller in 1965 things began to change, and by 1967 the channel had truly announced its arrival with the launch of a lavish drama – *The Forsyte Saga* starring Kenneth More and Eric Porter. It was considered a risky ploy at the time, but it was a gamble that paid off with an average audience of six million – not bad considering it was thought that only nine million people could access the channel at that time. Anyway, with programmes like *Play School* and *The Forsyte Saga*, it didn't seem to me that David Attenborough was a football fan or that BBC2 would be showing much of our favourite sport in the foreseeable future.

That left just BBC1 and ITV to provide us with our football kicks. So it came to pass that *The Big Match* and the genial face of Brian Moore arrived on our Sunday afternoon screens on 25 August 1968. Former BBC radio commentator Moore was joined by my 'old friend' Jimmy Hill who, as I mentioned earlier, could often come across as a figure of fun. *The Big Match* went some way in consolidating this image. Dad was never a big fan of commercial television and I don't believe it was just because the adverts would often get in the way of the programmes. As with many of my dad's causes, it was a matter of principle, and his opinion was that the BBC simply produced better programmes. He was correct in most cases and I suppose *The Big Match* was a good example of the dumbing-down of television. When the programme introduced a fun spot, it was rather like *Ski Sunday* – downhill all the way.

The choice of tune for the fun spot didn't help matters – a 1970 song by Albert Hammond and Mike Hazlewood called 'Gimme Dat Ding'. Hammond is an English Gibraltarian songwriter who, as a solo performer/writer, collaborated on a string of solo hits in the 1970s, including 'The Free Electric Band' and 'It Never Rains in Southern California'. He and Hazlewood also composed one of the great love songs, 'The Air That I Breathe', which was a huge worldwide hit for The Hollies. Unfortunately, 'Gimme Dat Ding' was one of those annoying novelty records of that period that you often find yourself singing out loud. Other examples of this genre include 'In The Summertime' by Mungo Jerry, 'Mouldy Old Dough' by Lieutenant Pigeon, as well as the whole Abba repertoire.

The song was performed by Roger Greenaway and Tony Burrows, better known as Pipkins. In some ways the song replicates Peter Sellers's take on Lonnie Donegan, when Sellers, in the guise of Lennie Goonigan, says: 'I've got rid of all the verses and made it one long chorus.' So in this case you are basically left with the lyric:

Gimme, Gimme Dat Ding
Gimme Dat, Gimme Dat
Gimme, Gimme, Gimme Dat
Gimme Dat Ding, Gimme Dat
Gimme, Gimme Dat, Gimme Dat Ding
Gimme Dat, Gimme, Gimme Dat,
Gimme, Gimme, Gimme, Dat Ding

To make it worse, the song is delivered in a high-pitched whine, reminiscent of most of Pinky and Perky's output. When *The Big Match* production team married this with a few seconds of recently recorded football footage, speeded up and repeated ad nauseam, you had the aforementioned fun spot. Oh how we laughed before turning over to BBC2 for The John Player one-day cricket match with Frank Bough, John Arlott and Jim 'I Don't Like One-Day Cricket' Laker.

It was little wonder football fans were often in need of an alternative outlet to watch football-related programmes on the telly. Luckily, BBC1's drama department and a young director – the Nuneaton-born, Bath City supporter Ken Loach – were to provide an unlikely and much-needed source of joy and authenticity. *The Golden Vision* is a typical Loach film, featuring documentary-style footage of a group of hard-nosed but loveable working-class Everton supporters to whom football is so much more than just a game. As their then adversary Bill Shankly would answer when asked whether football really was a matter of life and death; it was 'much more important than that'. These Everton fans put their team before anything else, including births, marriages and deaths ...

There's plenty of sharp Scouse wit, heated football discussions and sing-songs in the pub, as well as up close and personal match-day action featuring Everton's away game at Arsenal. The post-match trip to central London and the visit to a Soho strip club is particularly amusing, especially when the 'passionate and exciting Miss Mata Atari' arrives on stage looking rather like Eartha Kitt, accompanied by a piano, exotic birdsong and the sound of Ken Jones's character, Joe Horrigan, and his pals assessing Gordon West's fine performance in the Everton goal: 'He made some fantastic saves, but I think the greatest one he made was from Frank McLintock's shot that went like a rocket towards the onion bag. He got both hands to it and ended up in the net himself. Oh it was fantastic, that! But from the very early times we've always had very good centre-forwards. And now what about the feller we've got now, Alex Young, the Golden Vision …'

The drama includes shots of the players training as well as an interview with Alex Young himself. The pensive, softly-spoken Scot comes across as a normal, down-to-earth and vulnerable man. Although idolised by the fans, he seems unsure of himself and his own ability. Loach's skilful technique manages to put fan and footballer on the same level.

Loach was to feature football in his Yorkshire-based film, *Kes*, the following year. The film was voted the seventh-best British picture of the 20th century in a poll by the British Film Institute. Although the football scene is only eight minutes long, every second counts. It is one of the most memorable and amusing football sequences filmed, a brief escape from what is at times a bleak and moving film that portrays the young life of a 15-year-old schoolboy – Billy Casper, sympathetically played by David Bradley. Casper is bullied both at home and at school before finding temporary solace in his love for a kestrel.

Loach's interpretation of 'the beautiful game' really hits home, and the game's venue – a school field in Barnsley – will be familiar to most schoolchildren who have ever played or been forced to play the game on a desolate and depressing cold, wet, winter day. The boys seem uninterested and bored even before the bully of a schoolmaster – Mr Sugden, played quite beautifully by Brian Glover – arrives on the horizon, jogging enthusiastically, resplendent in a bright-red tracksuit, carrying a rock-hard ancient leather football and ref's whistle. You can tell immediately that Sugden, mentally still a child himself, means business. This is confirmed when he nominates a boy called Tibbut to be the other captain before picking the star player, Padgett, for his own team. When Tibbut protests that Padgett is one of the best players, Sugden puts him in his place: 'Do you want to play football or do some maths?'

The teams are then quickly chosen until just one boy remains; inevitably it's Casper, who Sugden is forced to have on his side. Playing with the wind and downhill, Sugden removes the tracksuit top to reveal a red Manchester United kit. When one of the opposition asks if Sugden is Liverpool today, he says: 'Don't you know your club colours, boy? Manchester United strip, this.' 'Are you playing as Denis Law?' 'No, Charlton today, lad, all over the field, too cold for striker.' 'Of course Charlton's not as good as Denis Law.' 'Are you trying to tell me about football? Anyway, Denis Law's in the wash this week.'

After learning that the opposition will be Spurs, Sugden multitasks, becoming the TV commentator too: 'So it's Manchester United versus Spurs in this important fifth-round cup tie at Old Trafford. And it's the fair-haired, slightly balding Charlton to kick off.' Sugden then, without passing, proceeds to clumsily progress up the field with the ball at his feet, barging one boy out the way before playing a through ball that leads to nothing. 'Come on, Speed, what are you playing at? You should have been on the move, it was straight to your feet!' Spurs then go up the other end to score past Casper, the hapless United goalkeeper, who gets the inevitable telling-off from his captain: 'I've never seen such slack work in my life, Casper.' He accompanies the ticking-off by throwing the sodden ball at Casper, knocking him off his feet into a huge puddle in the goalmouth. 'What's that for, sir?' Casper asks. 'Slack work, Casper,' Sugden replies.

Manchester United soon equalise when Sugden's Charlton theatrically dives and immediately awards himself a dubious penalty. Sugden/Charlton takes it, but not before he admonishes the defender, saying: 'Who do you think you are? Bremner?' The penalty is saved, but Sugden says the goalkeeper moved and retakes it to score. Cue wild celebrations from Sugden, who tells the boys: 'And that, boys, is how to take a penalty, look one way and kick it the other.' Sugden is now even more repugnant and he blatantly brings down Tibbut. When the boy complains, Sugden sends him off. Spurs are now a man short, but justice is eventually done when they score the winning goal.

The film was one of the first of several collaborations between Ken Loach and Barry Hines, who wrote the original novel, *A Kestrel for a Knave*, which used authentic Yorkshire dialect. The extras were all hired from the Barnsley area. The DVD version has certain scenes dubbed over, with fewer of the trickier to understand dialect terms than the original. In a 2013 interview Loach said that, upon its release, United Artists organised a screening of the film for some American executives, who said that they could understand Hungarian better than the dialect in the film!

Loach's hat-trick of fine football dramas is completed by the 2009 film *Looking for Eric*. Loach explains the ethos of the film: 'We wanted to deflate the idea of celebrities as more than human. And we wanted to make a film that was enjoying the idea of what you and I would call solidarity, but what others would call support for your friends really, and the old idea that we are stronger as a team than we are as individuals.'

Or as Eric Cantona puts it in the film, 'You have to trust your team-mates always. If not we are lost.'

Eric Bishop: "Sometimes we forget you are just a man."

Eric Cantona: "I am not a man, I am Cantona."

The film features many of the same themes used in *The Golden Vision* and *Kes*: a downtrodden frustrated hero in a rut trying unsuccessfully to make things better. In this film it is Eric Bishop and not Joe Horrigan or Billy Casper. Eric is a football-fanatic postman whose life is descending into crisis. By looking after his granddaughter he is coming into contact with his ex-wife, Lily, whom he abandoned after the birth of their daughter. Meanwhile, his stepson, Ryan, is hiding a gun under the floorboards of his bedroom for a violent drugs baron. As his life continues to spiral downwards, Bishop considers suicide. But after smoking cannabis with fellow postmen in his living room, his hallucinations bring forth his footballing hero, the famously philosophical Eric Cantona, who gives him advice, eventually becoming his life coach.

Thanks to Bishop's new imaginary pal, his relationship with his wife starts to improve dramatically. After finding the gun, he confronts Ryan who admits to his involvement with the drugs gang, and Bishop attempts to return the gun to the gangster. With his life now perilously in the balance, Bishop is advised by Cantona to seek help from his friends and to 'surprise' himself. Bishop organises 'Operation Cantona', sneaking dozens of fellow Manchester United fans – wearing Cantona masks and including Cantona himself – into the gangster's house and humiliating him and his family. The film ends at Bishop's daughter's graduation day, where the family reunites. Midway through the credits we see Cantona's famous press conference containing his memorable quote: 'When the seagulls follow the trawler, it's because they think sardines will be thrown into the sea.' Ooh ah Cantona indeed.

Another Sunday and Sweet F.A. by Jack Rosenthal is a 1972 drama for Granada TV. Rosenthal, one of my favourite writers, looks at grassroots football as seen through the eyes of Eric Armistead, a Manchester-based Sunday league referee played by David Swift. The opening tells it as it is going to be as we watch Eric leaving home on match day, unable to get through the front gate, which is blocked by two youths enjoying an early-morning fight. Eric calmly waits for the boys to move and, when they don't, gives them until the count of five to move. He patiently counts and, when they remain still grappling by the gate, quietly says 'six' to himself before doing a detour and climbing over the front garden wall to begin his walk to the ground.

Rosenthal says that for Armistead 'life is an immorality play. Right never triumphs over wrong. Good never vanquishes evil. No one knows the meaning of "fairness". Which is why he's a Sunday morning referee – hoping that in his own small way, in a foreign field that's forever Manchester, he and his whistle might change the world.' He referees a match between Sunday league teams Parker Street Bus Depot and CWS Albion 2nd XI and the idea seems to be that victory goes to the team that inflicts the most grievous bodily harm on the other. In the CWS penalty area, Graham, the Parker Street captain, weaves past three defenders, draws the goalkeeper and gently strokes the ball towards goal. It rolls nearer and nearer ... then stops two inches from the line. A defender races up and boots it out of play. Graham turns away miserably. Eric is nearby.

Graham: We should have had a cricket score.

Eric: That's life, lad.

Graham: Can't you just give us one?

Eric: And that's wishful thinking.

Graham: I think there's a jinx on that ball.

Eric: You can't blame the ball. Blame the patron saint of football.

Graham: Who's that?

Eric: Mephistopheles.

Graham: Who's that?

The game continues until in the last minute, with the whistle in Eric's mouth, a Parker Street player beats his full-back and makes to centre the ball. Eric, watching, sprints into the penalty area as the ball is centred, leaps into the air like a latter-day Dixie Dean and heads the ball like a rocket into the back of the net. He whistles for a goal, points to the centre circle and thrusts his hand in the air à la Denis Law. The impossible has happened. On a quiet Sunday morning in Manchester, the earth has spun to a stop and has started rotating in the opposite direction. The 22 players stare at Eric, dead-eyed, in utter incomprehension. Eric strides back towards the centre spot, noting the goal in his book and checking the time on his watch. All the players are standing stock-still, motionless since the moment he headed the ball.

Graham throws his hands up in the air and yells in jubilation. His team-mates follow suit and race about congratulating and kissing each other. On the touchline the Parker Street supporters cheer deliriously.

It slowly dawns on the CWS team what's happened. They converge on Eric in a jostling, pushing, angry mob – screaming, threatening and pleading their protests. In response he takes from his pocket a copy of the F.A. Laws of Football. He finds the relevant page.

Eric: Law 9, paragraph B of the Laws of Football published by the Council of the Football Association, Patron Her Majesty the Queen, states as follows: 'The ball is in play if it rebounds off either the referee or linesman when they are in the field of play.' Satisfied?

He replaces his booklet.

CWS Captain: Are we hell-as-like! It didn't rebound off you!

The rest of his team yell their agreement.

Eric (calmly): Don't argue with the referee, lads. I don't want to send you all off. They'd only stroll upfield and tap another one in, wouldn't they?

CWS Manager: Ref. The ball didn't rebound off you. You jumped up and headed the sodding thing in. Deliberate.

Rosenthal's bit of fun represents a kind of revenge for referees everywhere. It's madness but it makes some kind of sense for anyone who has played, been in charge of or watched a game of football.

Earlier I discussed in some detail the two teams at the centre of Sönke Wortmann's 2003 film *The Miracle of Bern* – Hungary and West Germany. The 1954 World Cup was held in Bern, Switzerland, and at that time Hungary were the top-ranked team in the world and red-hot favourites to win the trophy for the first time. The Mighty Magyars had not lost a game in four years, were the reigning Olympic Champions and had also won the Central European International Cup in 1953, the same year as the 6-3 demolition of England at Wembley. As the tournament progresses, Hungary play their usual confident game, beating South Korea 9-0 and then, significantly, West Germany 8-3.

There were two aspects of the latter game that are worth noting. Firstly, Hungary's talismanic star and captain, Ferenc Puskas, was injured when the German defender Liebrich caught his ankle from behind and Puskas was immediately taken off. 'I was not happy and remember in the dressing room our team doctor Laszlo Kreisz kept prodding my leg here and there,' Puskas explained. 'I told him to pour some cold water on it, and that it wouldn't get better with him just prodding it.' Secondly, West Germany manager Sepp Herberger played a weaker team, believing they could afford to lose to Hungary and still qualify. They did exactly that.

Meanwhile Hungary, minus Puskas, won both their final two qualifying games – 4-2 against Brazil and Uruguay. The Hungarians topped their group and were drawn to play Brazil once more in the quarter-final, still without Puskas. In a violent encounter known as 'The Battle of Bern' and refereed by Englishman Arthur Ellis, Hungary triumphed 4-2, but not before the Hungarian Kocsis and Brazil's Nílton Santos and Humberto Tozzi had been sent off. Hungary were rewarded with a semi-final encounter with Uruguay, which they won 4-2 after extra time, with Kocsis heading both the decisive goals. He was later to be named Best Player of the tournament. This game was described by many as the greatest game of football ever seen and had a unique finish when, 2-1 down, the Uruguayans equalised late on through Hohberg, who collapsed to the ground. The excitement of scoring such a vital goal was so great that he fainted. Meanwhile the unseeded West Germans beat Yugoslavia 2-0 in the quarter-final and progressed to the final by beating neighbours Austria 6-1.

Puskas was pronounced fit for the final, but the build-up to the match proved problematic for Hungary. The night before the final the Swiss national brass-band competition took place, with parades passing by the team's hotel until two in the morning as Hungarian manager Gusztáv Sebes explains: 'It was dreadful and to make it worse they started playing again just after lunch on the day of the final, when the players wanted an hour's sleep.'

The weather also didn't help Hungary. It rained all day before the final and very heavily in the second half of the match itself. For the German team and Sepp Herberger, it was a miracle. The rain, which so suited skipper Fritz Walter, slowed down the Hungarians. The whole West German team were also aided by Adolf Dassler's revolutionary new Adidas boots, fitted with screw-in studs.

The final, played in front of 60,000 fans, started well for Hungary. Puskas scored after six minutes and Zoltán Czibor got a second two minutes later. It looked like the tournament favourites were on their way, but Max Morlock pulled one back for the Germans within two minutes, and they equalised eight minutes after that through Helmut Rahn. In the pouring rain and thick mud of the second period, Hungary did everything possible to regain the lead, with Hidegkuti hitting the post, Kocsis the bar, and Kohlmeyer cleared off the line. Goalkeeper Turek also played his part, pulling off a string of great saves. But with just six minutes left, Rahm scored his second goal, a powerful low strike that skimmed off the sodden surface and past Grosics in the Hungary goal. There was still time for Puskas to score what Hungary thought was the equaliser, but it was controversially ruled out for offside.

In 1981 big-screen football fans had two vastly contrasting films on offer to tempt them to their local cinema: Bill Forsyth's *Gregory's Girl* and John Huston's *Escape to Victory*. The former is an easy-going comedy set in Cumbernauld, Scotland, featuring John Gordon Sinclair as Gregory Underwood, an awkward teenager who plays in his underachieving school football team. To improve things, the coach holds a trial to find new players. Dorothy, played by Dee Hepburn, turns out to be an excellent player, as well as very good-looking, and subsequently takes Gregory's place as centre-forward. Gregory, who is immediately smitten by Dorothy, doesn't mind a bit and is happy to play in goal.

Following advice from his precocious younger sister, Gregory tries to go out with Dorothy who, along with several of her friends, conspires to arrange a series of dates with nearly all of them but not Dorothy. Gregory is seen kissing with one of the girls, Susan, and seems to like her. Meanwhile Gregory's friends, Andy and Charlie, who have always failed with girls in the past, have seen him out with three separate girls and are deeply envious. As a result they plan a trip to Caracas, where Andy has heard women greatly outnumber the men. They fail with that too! Amongst all of this farcical behaviour there's some footy footage, mainly consisting of Gregory gawping at Dorothy prancing around the pitch in a pair of tiny, tight silk football shorts.

Escape to Victory is a kind of sporty remake of the prisoner of war breakout picture *The Great Escape*, but instead of Steve McQueen and Richard Attenborough we have Sylvester Stallone and Michael Caine, plus a back-up team of footballing extras including Pelé, Bobby Moore, Osvaldo Ardiles, Mike Summerbee and most of the Ipswich Town first-team squad.

In 1981 Caine and Stallone were two of the biggest box-office stars in the world. Stallone had just completed two of his six-strong set of boxing-themed *Rocky* films and was soon to get even nastier and richer when he morphed into *Rambo.* Caine meanwhile was approaching veteran status, having established himself in the 1960s with lead or co-lead roles in *Zulu*, *The Ipcress File*, *Alfie*, *Get Carter*, *The Italian Job* and my particular favourite, *Sleuth* – a two-man tour de force with Laurence Olivier.

The convoluted plot of *Escape to Victory* revolves around a planned escape from a German prisoner of war camp and a football match organised by English captain and former West Ham United player John Colby (Caine). The Allies, with Stallone in goal, will play a German team in an exhibition game in Paris. Stallone's performance, like some of his American football-style tackles, is completely over the top and Caine goes through the motions, replacing his famous *Italian Job* 'You're only supposed to blow the bloody doors off' routine with a somewhat limper line: 'You play in your American-style way and you'll be barred!'

As the voice-over in the film's publicity trailer put it: 'The Allied High Command called them crazy and maybe they were.' That might be true but the plot is crazier and the performances both on and off the pitch are poor. Not even Pelé can rescue it and *Gregory's Girl* wins hands down. Let's put it this way, who would any football-loving fan rather watch for nearly two hours, Dee Hepburn or Sylvester Stallone? Oh, the game finishes 4-4, in case you were wondering.

I must also mention probably the best soccer-themed TV advert ever: Carlsberg's 2006 take on Sunday morning football, *Old Lions.* First we see Peter Shilton yawning in bed, Peter Reid having a coffee, Alan Ball rummaging in the laundry basket for some clean football socks, and Peter Beardsley pedalling out of his garage on his bicycle. Next Jack Charlton picks up the lads in a battered builder's Transit van. The van is pretty full when he pulls up to collect Chris Waddle, who throws his gear in the back of the van as Charlton stop-starts the van a few times so he can't get in. Terry Butcher stops off for some bacon sarnies before shouting at Beardsley from the passenger window to 'get those little legs going'. Alan Ball then asks who they are playing and, when told it's the Dog and Duck, replies: 'I'll mark the dog.'

On arrival at the ramshackle ground there is much banter in the dressing room as the boys put on their England kit. Manager Bobby Robson then starts his team talk, only to be interrupted by a phone call from Stuart Pearce's mum. Once on the pitch, they receive some astonished looks from the opposition and their fans, before immediately scoring three goals without the other team getting a look-in. We then witness a tasty tackle from Peter Reid before Jack Charlton gets booked for shirt-pulling. Big Jack has brother Bobby by his side when the ref asks for his name. Peter Shilton finally has a save to make before three or four goals find their way into the opposition's net to make the final score 8-0. At the full-time whistle Bobby Robson shakes hands with the opposition's manager and players before telling Jack Charlton: 'Don't call me, I'll call you.' The team celebrate in the Dog and Duck pub, with the narrator providing the famous strapline: 'Carlsberg don't do pub teams. But if they did they'd probably be the best pub team in the world.'

Last but not least, *I Believe In Miracles* is director Jonny Owen's amusing and heartfelt 2015 documentary of how the egocentric and charismatic Brian Clough and his assistant Peter Taylor turned an assortment of down-and-out Nottingham Forest footballers into double European champions in 1979 and 1980. The story starts with Clough's sacking after just 44 days in charge of Leeds United in 1975. Clough is at rock bottom and his only job offer comes from Forest, then a run-down Second Division club who seem to be going nowhere. Clough has other ideas and the club go on to beat the world's best and become one of the greatest sides in British football history.

Adapted from journalist Daniel Taylor's book of the same name, the film features previously unseen match action, a fantastic 70s soundtrack of funk and soul tracks, and lengthy interviews with most of the players, including the highly amusing and much-feared centre-half duo of Kenny Burns and Larry Lloyd. It's a hilarious, inspirational, emotional epic. Or as *The Guardian* puts it: 'The greatest football film ever made.'

CHAPTER 7

Back Playing Again

WHEN MY attempts to play school football in glasses spectacularly and painfully failed, the game went on the back burner for a few years and a new group of non-sporty, rock-music-loving, concert-going, beer-drinking pals replaced it. I still watched and supported Watford, but most of my new school friends were not keen on the game. At the start they included Graeme Andrews, Alan Patterson and Steve Hutchins.

By the time I was in the sixth form, Michael Curson, Gill Harris and Dane Stevens also became friends. Alan Patterson liked football and we went to see several games together, including the memorable FA Cup tie against Manchester United at Old Trafford in 1969. Like me, they were all keen music fans. Alan's older brother, Bill, even had a temperamental 8-track tape player in his car. Up until this time I was mainly influenced by some of the sounds I heard on my mum's wireless at home and what I heard coming from Laurie's bedroom – mainly Cream, The Beatles, Yes, Keef Hartley, Graham Bond and an assortment of Tamla Motown and Chicago blues.

For a few years Graeme Andrews was my best mate and I would sometimes visit his parents' home in Leavesden directly after school to listen to records. I remember we discovered J.J. Cale together (not in person, obviously) and also Wishbone Ash and ZZ Top. We were both regular customers at Past and Present Records in north Watford, visiting the shop most Saturday mornings. We later formed a mobile disco, The East of St Louis Roadshow, named after the Duke Ellington song 'East St. Louis Toodle-Oo' that we had heard on Steely Dan's third album, *Pretzel Logic*. Steve Hutchins liked The Incredible String Band and also the silly and surreal Bonzo Dog Doo-Dah Band. Via Michael Curson I became a Neil Young fan, *Harvest* being one of the first LPs I bought. Michael also introduced me to cannabis and I enjoyed my first smoke in a park near his Abbots Langley home. We and a few others also enjoyed a lunchtime pint in his local pub, the Compasses. Gill Harris turned me on to Joni Mitchell and Carole King, and Dane Stevens was a singer and guitarist in a Yes-soundalike band called Druid. He hosted one or two great parties at his parents' home in King Street, Watford. One of them featured a pal of his playing boogie-woogie piano throughout the evening and the atmosphere, aided by copious amounts of beer and Spanish brandy, was fantastic. I also remember Dane and drummer Cedric 'Sid' Sharpley coming back to Bricket Wood after a few pints in Watford and attacking Dad's drinks cabinet; the Dimple whisky receiving a severe pasting as I recall. Luckily they didn't take the bottle with them and Dad used it to keep sixpences in, as a kind of memento. South African-born Cedric went on to be Gary Numan's drummer in his band Tubeway Army and tragically died of a heart attack in 2012, aged 59.

A year or so after I left school I started playing tennis at Townsend Tennis Club in St Albans. It was the summer of 1977 and one of the first people I met was a lad named Ian Stuart, who was around my age and soon became a good friend. We got on well and played tennis together on a regular basis in weekend and midweek club matches. After a few months Ian mentioned that he played football for a local side called St Albans Wanderers. He asked me if I was a footballer and I told him I used to play but that my eyesight wasn't great and I didn't feel comfortable playing in glasses. He then delicately rummaged around in his right eye and then the left and said: 'Contact lenses. I'm as blind as a bat and have been playing football in them for a couple of years now.'

Within a few months I was Bricket Wood's answer to Nobby Stiles as I sported a pair of hard lenses that were uncomfortable, extremely tricky to insert and had a tendency to pop out of my eye at any blinking moment, whether I was playing football or not. However, they had one thing going for them: I could see pretty well and my football career was back on track. I was sure that both Matt Busby and the new Watford manager, Graham Taylor, would soon be on a scouting mission to take a look at me at Westminster Lodge before you could say Baden-Powell.

I joined Ian, who looked and played football like Trevor Brooking, and several other Townsend tennis players who were members of the club, and began playing for the Saturday second team, the Strollers. It was an important moment for me, introducing me not only to a great club but also myriad characters, a few scoundrels and some players who have since become lifelong friends. One of these was Geoff Watts, a teacher at Francis Bacon School in St Albans. Here's his account of our first meeting: 'I first encountered St Albans Wanderers as an opponent. In 1977 I was playing for a side called Alban and lined up against the Wanderers, marking a tall fast winger. About ten minutes into the game I turned to find him on the ground, clutching his face. I was rather concerned that the referee would interpret this as an unsavoury "off the ball" incident and take severe action against me. I was quick to point out that I had not touched him and had done nothing to cause whatever injury he had sustained. I thought it best not to add that I would have been delighted to have been able to summon up enough speed to get anywhere near enough to stop him by any means, legal or otherwise.

'As we approached to find out what was going on, it emerged that he hadn't been diving or play-acting (there wasn't much of that sort of thing in 1977) – he had lost a contact lens. Sympathy then took over from suspicion and there followed one of the more bizarre scenes I have ever witnessed in parks football – 22 players and a referee on their hands and knees, crawling round on a small patch of grass trying to find the missing lens. I have often wondered how this was viewed by the Saturday afternoon public taking their leisure in Verulamium Park. After all, not even in church leagues is it normal for games to be suspended for an impromptu prayer meeting. Such was my first meeting with the author of this book.' I never did find that bloody lens, Geoff, but I carried on playing with one eye and had a blinder!

I played on the right wing for the first few seasons with the club, but when I began playing on Sunday mornings for the second team, managed by a tall, well-built character called Jeff Harber, I was moved to right-back. Jeff, or 'Loafer' as he was known, could see I had potential in that position. At the time I doubted him, but he proved to be correct. I was initially concerned that I would spend all my time in my own half defending, and that's how it was at the beginning. However, I was fortunate that the fellow playing directly in front of me was the ponderous and mainly defensive-minded Barry Atkinson. Barry might not have had much flair or pace, but he was dependable and a good team player. Gradually I started to overlap and I instructed Barry to cover me. In time Barry got used to this and I often spent more time attacking than defending. In one game against The Queen's Head in Sandridge, I found myself in their penalty area with the ball at my feet approximately 15 seconds into the match. I shot wide, but I'd like to believe it's the thought, as well as my attacking intentions, that counts. Later on in my 19-year career with the Wanderers I also played as a target man and even made one or two appearances at centre-half. Never in goal or in midfield; I was not brave enough for the former or fit enough for the latter …

A character I met early on at the club was a Stan Bowles lookalike named Kenny Burtenshaw. It was one of my first appearances and Kenny, fashionably late, strolled into the dark and dingy dressing room and immediately lit up a grey winter afternoon with a pre-match ciggie and his unusual behaviour. He unpacked his rucksack (no sports bag for him) and started singing, unnecessarily loudly, the words to 'Psycho Killer': 'I can't seem to face up to the fact, I'm tense and nervous and I can't relax, I can't sleep 'cause my bed's on fire, don't touch me I'm a real live wire, Psycho Killer …' This alarming and rather unsettling impersonation of the band's eccentric and, on this song, menacing lead singer, David Byrne, was not only my introduction to Kenny but Talking Heads as well.

'What have we got here?' I thought. This seminal single, to my knowledge, had not yet been released so I presumed Kenny must have heard it in a club the previous night. After all, as I was later to learn, Kenny was an art director at a London advertising agency. As an innocent youth still living at home, it seemed to me that he enjoyed a more exotic and cosmopolitan lifestyle. He had to travel in from London by train from his own house in Maida Vale, for a start! You can't get much more cosmopolitan than that.

I was a little overawed by this performance and looked around the dressing room at my team-mates, none of whom, apart from Ian, I knew. They looked as though they hadn't a clue who Talking Heads were and, more interestingly, none took a blind bit of notice of Kenny's antics. They looked like a bunch of grizzled veterans who groaned, coughed and spluttered before going back to their roll-ups. They seemed well used to Kenny's antics. Once the game began, everything started to make sense. Playing very loosely on the left side of midfield, Kenny was all left foot, drag-backs and pirouettes. He was undoubtedly talented, but he seemed to shuffle rather than run and would often be travelling in the wrong direction. Kenny was in need of a soccer satnav system as he wandered in strange circular motions around the pitch as if he had been raised by a family of Navajo Indians in Arizona and not, as it turned out, by his mum in Welwyn Garden City. Our defenders would start pleading with him either to pass or at least head off towards the opponents' half. These requests would mainly fall on deaf ears. In many ways Kenny was ahead of his time. Skilful, as well as comfortable and relaxed on the ball, he would think nothing of keeping possession in tight spaces, near his own goal. In some ways he was a prototype Andrés Iniesta.

The problem was that Kenny wasn't as good as Iniesta and we were definitely not Barcelona. I doubt if many of us had even heard of Barcelona, let alone been there. The other problem was that Kenny didn't have much pace and couldn't tackle a fish supper so, if he lost the ball, he had no chance of getting it back. Veteran Wanderer Peter Lingham recalls one of his early matches: 'I was playing at full-back and heard Kenny calling for the ball 20 yards ahead of me. I looked up to see him surrounded by three opponents. I thought, OK, you know best, and pinged the ball towards him at pace. He controlled it in an instant, dropped his shoulder and left his markers for dead, meandering off down the wing. I said to my fellow defender, Brian Weatherer, "What a marvellous game this can be."'

Kenny is a lovely fellow and had many friends at the club. However, his style of play wasn't appreciated by everyone. Club chairman Jake Ewing, for instance, couldn't understand the way Kenny played football. He and Kenny were poles apart and to witness Jake on the touchline while Kenny was in possession and in his pomp was always a joy. Jake, who was in his mid to late 70s then, would often say something like: 'Just kick the bloody thing, Burtenshaw!' To him football really was that simple. Kenny was a maverick and played the game his way, and I think we all secretly admired him.

Michael Cooper, a handy footballer for the Wanderers and a good cricketer for St Albans, tells an amusing tale that epitomises Jake's infamous touchline antics: 'Jake literally kicked and headed every ball when watching the Wanderers. During one away game against one of the many St Albans-based psychiatric hospitals – take your pick from Cell Barnes, Hill End, Harperbury, Napsbury or Shenley – Jake was closely observed by one of the staff of the hospital who was watching the game too. At the final whistle the gentleman went up to Jake and, taking him firmly by the arm, started to lead him back inside the hospital. Jake started pleading with him: "No, I'm the manager of the visiting team!" he cried. "Of course you are, sir, they all say that," was the reply.

'Luckily for Jake, one or two of our players managed to persuade the conscientious member of staff that Jake was indeed our leader and not an inmate. Jake made it home to his wife, Hilda, and didn't have to spend the night in a straightjacket in a padded cell. Jake would probably have said that some of the football we played drove him mad! I have since learned that one of the original club members, Geoff Evans, was in medical records and organised many early White Hart Wanderers friendlies against the hospital teams. At times Jake ran the club with an iron fist. Opinionated and oversimplistic maybe, but he mixed that with an equal sprinkling of passion and dedication. The club was his life and all grassroots football clubs need a Jake to be able to survive and flourish.'

Jon Berry, who made his debut for the Wanderers in 1981, remembers Kenny with some affection: 'Burtenshaw was, in those days, something of a dandy, with flowing, fashionable locks that were just on the turn to, let us say, silver. Having had enough of a whippersnapper trying, largely successfully, to run round him all afternoon, Kenny lost patience and clattered the poor youth, who picked himself up, looked Kenny in the eye and, rather uncharitably in my view, called him a "fat, grey-haired old wanker". To his eternal credit, Burtenshaw snapped back, without a moment's hesitation – "Oy, less of the old."'

Kenny's real claim to fame was scoring THE own goal to end all own goals. I didn't witness it myself, but Geoff Watts did. Here's Geoff's account of what happened on that famous afternoon in March 1979: 'Some games stick in the memory long after others have faded. This particular one, I would have remembered anyway as it was only my second one for the club and my first for the first team (the selection committee presumably having been deceived by some enthusiastic running-around in the reserves the week before). I'd never met any of the players before and was grateful that many went out of their way to make me feel at home. Ken's introduction of himself was followed by, "You'll have to remember that I'm totally one-footed." At the time I assumed that he was being modest. Early in the second half we were coasting to victory, 3-1 up. I was feeling more confident and was pleased to score the last one myself (a cross that the goalkeeper missed). Then came the show-stopper. Ken received the ball on the left touchline near the halfway line. Under pressure, he turned inside his man and began to head directly across the field. To shield the ball as further opponents joined in the fun, he twisted and turned until he was facing directly towards his own goal. A lesser player would have opted for a simple pass, but simplicity has never been Ken's style. Picture the scene then as he approached his own penalty area, ball still under perfect control, but looking like a latter-day Pied Piper as he was pursued by hordes of perplexed but determined opponents.

'John Barber in goal, never one to get overexcited, came off his line, shouting something like "Kenny, please give me the ball." To an individualist like Ken, the sight of goal and the goalkeeper off his line is a challenge that cannot be resisted.

The chip was perfection. In all my life playing and watching football, it is the only time I have ever seen the scoring of a goal produce no reaction from either side. There were no celebrations from the opposition, nor were there any recriminations among the defence. Everybody stood for a few moments. Nobody knew what to say. Everybody wondered if they were dreaming. The only movement was that of the drips of water falling from the netting where they had been disturbed, onto the ball nestling by the stanchion, right in the corner. When the game restarted we were only a goal in front and understandably panic-stricken. I've never seen Ken do so much work – tackling, chasing, pressurising – as he did in those next 20 minutes. It was all right in the end; we got another goal and won 4-2, but the talking point afterwards was not the result.

'There are moments in football that are special. For example, I do not believe that I will ever see a save better than Gordon Banks's from Pelé in the 1970 World Cup. Similarly, I don't think I will ever see a better own goal than Kenny's. When they show the clips of the half-dozen best own goals of the season on TV, others split their sides laughing. For myself, I don't get the enjoyment from them that I once did. I manage only a thin smile at the succession of sliced clearances, miscued back passes and wandering goalkeepers. I shake my head and mutter, "There'll never be another like Kenny's."'

After about a season of playing out on the right wing, I found myself, along with Ian and Kenny, on the fringe of the Saturday first team, which was then in the second tier of the Mid Herts League and contained some useful players like Paul and Brian Gathern, Mike O'Shea, Roger French, Barry Dawson, Mike Cooper, Geoff Foss, Colin Fassnidge and Todmorden-born Burnley fan Roly Newell, amongst others. Much of the attacking impetus of the team came from Paul Gathern and Roly. Paul was all left foot and a natural and consistent goalscorer. Although fairly small and slim, he was able to dance over the most muddy of midwinter soggy suet surfaces, leaving defenders in his wake. Many of Paul's mazy counter-attacking dribbles started from somewhere near the centre circle and ended with the ball being planted in the corner of the net.

Roly was, if anything, smaller than Paul and quite possibly the best ball-playing winger the club possessed. Roly's real skill was to wriggle his way down the flank before dinking a cross when only inches from the byline. Nimble, with quick feet, he was a centre-forward's dream and many were presented with simple tap-ins and headers. God forbid if you missed the target though. I once missed a simple header from one of Roly's marvellous crosses. I did everything right, drifting to the back post where, sure enough, Roly chipped the ball right on my head. It was a sitter. However, I headed wide from about eight yards and Roly, to his credit, said nowt. But when I sheepishly looked over to him, while the goalkeeper was preparing to take the goal kick, I could clearly see Roly running back shaking his head and mumbling obscenities to himself.

I think even Roly would admit that he had a bit of a temper on him, and this occasionally came to the surface, both on and off the pitch. There was one memorable occasion in the dressing room after a first-team defeat that sticks in my mind and makes stories of Alex Ferguson's hairdryer and tea cup tantrums pale into insignificance. I feel certain that 'Towelgate', as it became known, is now the benchmark for post-match football altercations. Roly's partner in this sordid story was, almost inevitably, Ken Burtenshaw. Showers were about to be taken and Roly was searching for his towel. He soon found it in the crowded cubicle that passed as a dressing room. It was on the dirty floor and, what was worse, Kenny's muddy football boot, still attached to Kenny's muddy left leg, was standing on a small corner of Roly's towel.

'You're standing on my towel, Burtenshaw!' Roly exclaimed. 'Oh,' Kenny replied innocently. Roly repeated his original remark, only with a little more venom: 'You're standing on my bloody towel! You'll never play for this club again, Burtenshaw!' By this time the room fell silent and a mix of mirth and unease filled the place. Roly was obviously serious, but we could all see the funny side. Unfortunately Roly couldn't, and, snatching his soiled towel, he grumpily made his way to the showers. I don't think Roly ever forgave Kenny, who, you will be heartened to hear, went on to play for the club on a regular basis for several more seasons.

In later years Roly would recount how he came to play for the Wanderers. In the early 1970s he was playing for Birkbeck College in Greenford, west London, and the standard was, in Roly's words, 'pretty decent'. The Wanderers had arranged a tour to Holland and were a few players short. Roly, who was living in St Albans at the time, had visited Townsend Tennis Club a few times and got to know Jeff Harber, Geoff Foss and Colin Fassnidge. They asked him if he could make the trip to Holland and Roly agreed. A short while afterwards, Roly, tired of the long journey to Greenford, decided to try and find a club nearer home. As Jeff, Geoff and Colin were playing for the Wanderers, they invited Roly to join them.

'It was a grey and damp winter's afternoon and, being the new boy, I arrived early for the Strollers' away game at

Cell Barnes,' Roly remembers. 'The first thing I saw were a couple of old wooden sheds beside the pitch that I assumed must be the changing rooms. I have to say I was starting to get worried.' Things were only to get worse when Roly entered the away team's shed. 'I was greeted by a middle-aged man, who turned out to be a farmer from Bricket Wood named Johnny Beha, being strapped into a corset by a couple of team-mates. I thought, "Bloody hell, what am I getting myself into?"' By the time the game began, things went from bad to worse for Roly. 'I almost got sent off after getting into a fight with a copper from Cell Barnes. Luckily, Mike Ewing acted as my minder and had a quiet word with Mr Plod.'

Roly's footballing prowess must have shined through as he immediately found his way into the first team the following week and proved to be a regular and dedicated club member. Roly's dedication was to be tested five years later when his father was made Mayor of Todmorden and he had to attend the accompanying civic ceremony one Friday afternoon and evening. No doubt several ales were sunk, but Roly manfully made the near 200-mile trip back to St Albans for the Saturday first-team game. 'I got to the ground just in time for kick-off and about 15 minutes in I was sent off for using bad language,' Roly explained. 'I pleaded with the ref that it was a private conversation as I was talking to a team-mate – Paul Gathern. I was upset as I didn't receive a pass from him and told him he was a greedy so-and-so. But the ref wouldn't listen, so I drove for five hours for a quarter of an hour's football. I think I got fined as well!' Whilst managing the Saturday first team in the late 1980s, it was Roly's duty to present the trophy for Player of the Year. His brief speech was priceless. 'The recipient of this award has all the five As:

attitude, ability, adaptability, availability … Avery.' Mark Avery duly stepped up to receive his just reward.

Gordon Murray moved south to St Albans from his home in Renfrew, west of Glasgow, in 1980, when he was 20, to work for British Aerospace in Hatfield. A keen footballer, Gordon played for youth side Renfrew YMCA as a teenager, and found his way to the Wanderers, like so many before him, via St Albans Cricket Club. 'Jake saw me playing cricket and when he discovered I was a keen footballer I joined the Wanderers soon after,' Gordon explained. 'I began playing at centre-half, observing the strange shape and size of my fellow defenders. But when I carried the ball out of defence and found myself over the halfway line, Jake decided midfield was my best position.' Gordon quickly adapted to football down south and recalls one of the advantages was the playing surface: 'The pitches were so much better down here. We always seemed to be playing on mud heaps in Renfrewshire.' However, communicating with his team-mates often caused problems for Gordon: 'I remember John Beattie shouting at me to "jockey, jockey, Gordon" when I was challenging an opponent. I didn't have a clue what he was on about, I thought he was insulting me! That expression doesn't exist in Scotland.' Throw-ins also caused confusion. 'We call a throw-in a "shy" and I'd never heard the English version before.'

Last word goes to Alan Garofall, in my opinion the most talented Wanderer of the lot. I once saw Alan score a sublime half-volley on the main pitch at Westminster Lodge one Sunday morning. The opposition goalkeeper made a bit of a hash of his goal kick and the ball fell to Alan some 30 yards out. He hit it first time and it flew into the top corner before you could blink.

'My overall memory is of what fantastic fun we had. I never played for another club that I enjoyed so much. We were talented, educated and played the game in the right way. I remember playing wonderful one-touch football on misty autumn mornings on the University College ground at London Colney, and Peter "Mardelli" Mardle as a young man with great pace and a terrific shot. I recall him scoring after seven seconds after he and I played five wall-passes through the opposition.

'Of course Jake's behaviour was capable of providing moments of memorable hilarity. One post-match lunchtime at the Lower Red Lion sticks in my mind. It was in the early 1970s, when we were all under threat of terrorist attacks. Jake left his large ex-military tea thermos outside the pub and it was almost destroyed in a controlled explosion as it was mistaken for an IRA bomb. Police were summoned and subsequently closed the road. They were about to call the bomb squad before Jake butted in: "Oh, you've found my tea urn – I wondered where I left it!"'

When Alan says he enjoyed his time at the Wanderers, the only Sunday club he played for, that's quite a compliment, because his list of clubs is impressive. In chronological order they are: Old Latymerians (an old school side that played in the Southern Amateur League), Oxford City, Oxford University, Tooting & Mitcham, Bishop's Stortford, Hertford Town, Hitchin Town, Aylesbury Town, Hemel Hempstead Town, Leighton Buzzard (now Leighton Town) and St Albans Wanderers. Alan also played at Wembley in 1966 and is the last Oxford Blue to score at each end in the Varsity Match played at Wembley.

Dad's father Alfred Bishop celebrating his 80th birthday. Auntie Joan and my brother Laurie look on

My parents' wedding day, 25 September 1948, at St. Gabriel's Parish Church, Bounds Green Road, London N22. Left to right: Alfred Bishop, Joan Francis, Geoff and Joyce Bishop, Nancy and Fred Hockey. Standing at the back is Ralph Bishop

Harry's hero: Harry with Ismaila Sarr

Yours truly, left in middle row, with Mount Pleasant Lane team-mates

Daddy's hero: Me and Luther Blissett enjoying a post-match photo opportunity

Ever the scribe: My uncle Jack in typical 'journo' pose

Dad enjoying a seasonal light ale

Heading for glory: A young Luther Blissett and John Barnes

My parents when I was just a twinkle in their eye

Father and son enjoying a well-earned drink with Isidre Ramon Madir and his son Marc after the Burnley defeat

Harry at Brentford before the game against Celta Vigo

St Albans Wanderers before their game against SV Leiselheim in August 1984

Pacemaker: I had a bit of speed back then ...

CHAPTER 8

Into Europe

WATFORD MAY have played in Europe in 1983 when they qualified for the UEFA Cup – or the wafer cup as my former mother-in-law used to say – but I did it five years earlier, representing St Albans Wanderers in a game against SV Leiselheim. Leiselheim is a small town near Worms in Germany's Upper Rhine region. St Albans' twin town in Germany was Worms, so St Albans Wanderers were chosen to represent the city and visit the area in the mid-70s. All players and club representatives have chairman Jack Ewing to thank for these marvellous two-way trips abroad, as Wanderers' stalwart and scribe Peter Lingham explains: 'Towards the end of his working life, coppersmith Jack was a shop steward in the de Havilland plant at Hatfield. In the course of industrial negotiations Jack was invariably party to feisty confrontations with a representative of management; so much so that in time a personal respect developed … Jack's "opponent" also had a place on the St Albans City Council, which received a request for a local football club to entertain a touring party under the "Town Twinning" scheme: the gig was offered to Jack and the Wanderers.

'The first visit from SV Leiselheim took place in 1972, followed by the reciprocal tour two years later in 1974. We went by rail, via Victoria, and soon developed a hero-worship for our team-mate, Dickie Warman, out of respect for his ability to speak German. As ever with the Wanderers, travel arrangements were subject to incidents. Changing trains at Köln proved to be a problem when the party contrived to split, several remaining on the platform, the rest on the train. Luckily the level-headed Ron Spiking organised a recovery to reunite the party further down the line.'

This situation was understandable in those days before mobile phones. Teams would often mislay players for away games in Redbourn or Welwyn Garden City, so what chance did we have, trying to negotiate the 500-mile trip to Worms! Subsequent tours were improved and squads kept intact when the decision was made to travel by coach and ferry. That was the journey I made in 1978. The five-day August bank holiday trip cost £40 and, once at our destination, we were put up by local families. I was lucky enough to stay at the marvellous 18th-century farmhouse of Alfred and Renate Bolian in the village of Pfeddersheim. Alfred was, and still is, an amusing, intelligent and warm-natured man. A teacher of economics at the local college in Worms, he played football in a calm and cultured manner. Alfred and his team-mates had learnt to play the ball to feet, partly as that was how they were taught to play and partly because they played on a hard shale pitch. This was because the club were not permitted to waste water maintaining a grass pitch; all the available water was used to help fertilise the grapes for the local wine.

The Wanderers would take around 40 people on the trip, most travelling on the coach with a few taking their own cars. We would leave early on the Friday morning and arrive late that night or in the early hours next day. Our reserves would take on a veterans team from SV Leiselheim on the Saturday afternoon, and afterwards a welcoming party and meal in the clubhouse would took place. We would be well-watered and fed and the party would often stretch into the early hours, which was fine, except that on the Sunday morning our first team would play Leiselheim's first team. We needed to be at our best and Jake would emphasise that we should go easy on the booze during the Saturday evening. No chance. Quite often we would gather bleary-eyed, bright and early at the ground, only to find one or two players were missing, having overdone it on a cocktail of German lager, wine and Schnapps. It's easy to forget that during this period, pre-match preparations consisted of a quick fag and a bit of coughing, and stretching to see what was available in the medical box. For many years the two or three Elastoplasts, bandages and tub of vapour rub were kept in a white toolbox with a red cross, made of red electrical tape, on the side. Also inside the box was a small glass bottle of horse liniment, also known as embrocation, which was mainly used by senior players who would energetically rub it on their legs just before kick-off. Peter Mardle would also carefully smear some vapour rub up his nostrils, followed by a larger amount rubbed onto his chest. I know the Welsh rugby union player, Cliff Morgan, was a big fan of embrocation, once saying: 'We might not be fit but we may as well smell fit.'

Luckily most of the reserves would turn up to watch the game and whoever could walk in a reasonably straight line was quickly drafted into the first team with a detailed, technical and tactical briefing: 'Do your best, we're in the blue shirts.' We might have done our best, but the situation wasn't improved when we ran out to see 11 fresh-faced fit-looking individuals we'd never seen before. They certainly hadn't been partying with us the previous night. We inevitably lost but received genuine post-match praise from the locals for putting on such a good show, under the circumstances. I took part in four trips to play SV Leiselheim on their testing pitch, the final one producing the one and only victory when Mark Avery scored the winner – a sweetly hit low shot from 25 yards that travelled through and past six or seven pairs of legs into the corner of an unsighted goalkeeper's net. Boy, did we celebrate!

There would also be celebrations at the wine-tasting trip held at Marliese and Egon Prior's establishment. This event would invariably be a testing time for our travelling translator, Marga Fagan. What would start off as a calm, relaxed and genial experience would rapidly disintegrate into drunken chaos. Before the wine-tasting began each person would be provided with the full list of the dozen or so wines to be sampled. All went smoothly, with Marga informing us, 'Wine number one, number eleven on your list, is a Leitz Weingut Rüdesheimer Riesling with a lively balance of apples, pears and peach.' Cue rapid quaffing of wine number one. Back to Marga: 'Wine number two, number seven on your list, is a 1975 Domdechant Werner Hochheimer Riesling with a mix of apple and pear offset by a tight zip of acidity.' Tasters: 'Prost!' Marga: 'Wine number three, number 11 on your list, is a 1970 Heinrichshof Sonnenuhr Riesling Trockenbeerenauslese offering unctuous apricot and fresh orange marmalade with trademark Mosel mineral texture exploding on your parrot.' Tasters: 'Polly Parrot!' Marga (now beginning to sway a bit in the 35-degree mid-afternoon heat): 'Wine number twelve and (rummaging around with her list) not sure the numbersch, Fräulein Prior, vot isdenumberschzz?' Tasters (not a care in the world what the number might be): 'Cheers, Big Ears!' Marga (tittering to herself): 'Wine number sixty, number sixteen on your list, is a fruity little numberzzzzzz.'

Everybody back in the coach! Yes, the final day of our trip was spent at the Backfischfest in Worms, a half-hour coach trip away from our digs. The Germans know how to have a party and this one was a cracker, combining wine, lager, traditional carnival rides and the mother of street processions involving much sweet-throwing from the floats into the crowds.

The Wormser Backfischfest is a tradition-rich festival that was first staged in 1933 and then forced into temporary retirement with war looming in 1939. Many of the rituals repeated here hark back to a place in time when Worms' citizens depended on the mighty Rhine to make their living. Part of the festival plays out on the ancient narrow street known as the Fischerwääd, the traditional home of the town's fishermen since 1106. This is the largest folk and wine festival held along the Rhine and has a curious double meaning. 'Backfisch' not only refers to a type of fried white fish, it's also an old slang expression for an innocent adolescent girl.

There's a nice tale involving Roly Newell and Jake during one of the first trips to Leiselheim. Roly was calming his nerves with a few drinks during a particularly bumpy ferry crossing from Dover. 'Jake, I'm not feeling too good,' a pale and sickly-looking Roly bleated. Jake happened to have some sea-sickness tablets and, after glancing at the bottle in the gloom, gave Roly a couple of them. Within a few minutes Roly was out like a light, sleeping like a baby. Jake, no doubt feeling pleased and proud of his medical expertise, took another look at the medicine bottle before going pale himself. It read: 'On no account should these tablets be taken whilst drinking alcohol.'

CHAPTER 9

Sounds Like Elton

REGINALD DWIGHT was born in Pinner, just a few miles south of Watford, on 25 March 1947. Encouraged by his musical parents, particularly his trumpet-playing father, Stan, he began playing the piano at a young age. By the time he was seven he was performing at parties and family gatherings, as well as taking formal piano lessons. He continued to show musical aptitude at school, including the ability to compose melodies, gaining some notoriety by playing like Jerry Lee Lewis at school functions. By the time he was 11, he won a junior scholarship to the Royal Academy of Music. Although he enjoyed playing classical piano pieces, particularly those of Chopin and Bach, he became a fan of rock and roll stars Elvis Presley and Bill Haley, and later the 'pounding' piano style of Little Richard. Despite Stan's wishes for him to become a banker, Reg chose music as a career and when he was 15 he was hired as a pianist at a nearby pub, the Northwood Hills Hotel, playing Thursday to Sunday nights. There he covered a range of popular standards, including songs by Jim Reeves and Ray Charles, as well as a few of his own compositions.

Reg, together with some friends, formed a band called Bluesology in 1962. By the mid-1960s, Bluesology was backing touring American soul and R&B musicians, including The Isley Brothers, and in 1966 they became Long John Baldry's backing band, playing regularly at London's Marquee Club. At around this time a former Highgate gravedigger, vocalist, harmonica player and mod by the name of Rod Stewart was playing with Baldry's band, and Reg and Stewart became acquainted, sometimes playing together.

In 1967 Reg answered an advertisement in the *New Musical Express* that led to him working with lyricist Bernie Taupin. The writing partnership started with Taupin sending Reg lyrics, to which he wrote the music. When the two first met later that year, they recorded their first song, 'Scarecrow'. Six months later Reg started to be known as Elton John, after two members of Bluesology – sax player Elton Dean and singer Long John Baldry. He legally changed his name to Elton Hercules John at the beginning of 1972. The newly formed writing team joined Dick James's DJM Records as staff songwriters in 1968, and over the next two years wrote material for various artists, among them a song for Lulu called 'I Can't Go On (Living Without You)', which finished sixth in the 1969 Eurovision Song Contest.

Elton had supported Watford since he was a boy and would travel up from Pinner to watch the game before staying with his dad in Croxley Green. This was in 1959, during the Cliff Holton era. Elton had a famous footballing uncle, Roy Dwight, who played for Fulham and then Nottingham Forest. Indeed Roy scored the opening goal in the 1959 FA

Cup Final against our rivals Luton Town at Wembley. Forest went on to win 2-1, but Dwight sustained a broken leg after a tackle from Luton's Brendan McNally, just after the half-hour mark, and was never the same player again. Having seen Elton play in kickabouts at Vicarage Road, I can safely say he didn't inherit many of Roy's soccer genes.

But he did want to get involved with the club in some way and, in the summer of 1973, with a prompt from his management team and some help from Oliver Phillips at the *Watford Observer*, Elton arrived at the club for a meeting with chairman Jim Bonser, a Lancashire-born construction magnate, the board and secretary Ron Rollitt. 'Before the meeting I advised Elton not to mention any figures as Bonser had developed a reputation of scaring off any newcomers that might pose a threat to him,' Phillips explained. Elton arrived in a pair of enormous platform-soled boots and played ball. He also suggested that his association with Watford would be good publicity for them and that a concert in aid of the club the following year might be a good idea. The board and Bonser agreed and Elton left as a signed-up vice president of the club, but not before taking a look around the ground and posing for photos for the following week's local paper. These included a shot of Elton in the players' dressing room with manager Mike Keen and the team. As it turned out, Elton got heavily involved with the club quicker than anyone anticipated when Bonser resigned in 1976 and Elton took his place.

By the time Elton, Rod Stewart and Nazareth showed up at the club for Elton's Country Comfort fundraising gig in May 1974, he was already one of the biggest pop stars in the world. He had released seven albums, including *Honky*

Château, *Don't Shoot Me I'm Only The Piano Player* and *Goodbye Yellow Brick Road*. *Honky Château* was his first US number-one album and *Don't Shoot Me* … reached number one in the UK, the US and Australia, among other countries. *Goodbye Yellow Brick Road* also topped the US and UK album charts for several weeks. In addition, Elton was touring the USA extensively over this period …

A big crowd had gathered at Vicarage Road to see Scottish rockers Nazareth open the show before Elton and his band played a set that included 'Daniel', 'Bennie and the Jets' and a few more of his hits. Rod Stewart also chipped in by singing along with Elton on 'Country Comfort', before going solo on 'Little Wing' and 'Sweet Little Rock 'n' Roller'. Everyone had a great time and the club received a cheque for £35,000 a few days later. 'I remember Jim Bonser's reaction when the cheque was handed over was one of disappointment,' Oliver Phillips recalled. 'He said he was hoping for £10,000 more!'

Elton John and his band were at their peak in 1974, a well-oiled music machine in concert and on record. His stage shows – which I witnessed three times around this time, including the Vic gig – were explosive affairs with Elton hell-bent on emulating his two piano heroes, Jerry Lee Lewis and Little Richard, in stage presence, musicianship and showmanship. And he didn't disappoint. Backing him were Davey Johnstone on guitar, Dee Murray on bass, Nigel Olsson on drums and rampant Ray Cooper on percussion. The following year he released my favourite album of his, *Captain Fantastic and the Brown Dirt Cowboy*, an autobiographical account of his (Captain Fantastic) and Bernie Taupin's (the Brown Dirt Cowboy) early days. It hit the top of the US Billboard chart within a week of its release, the first-ever album to do so, selling 1.4 million copies within four days. It was also certified gold based on pre-release orders in early May 1975. In 2003 *Rolling Stone* magazine ranked it number 158 on their list of the greatest 500 albums of all time. My only surprise is that it should have been higher.

It wasn't only Elton and the band who were flying at this time; Taupin's lyrics hit the mark too. Take the closing verse of the title track:

'And all this talk of Jesus coming back to see us couldn't fool us.
For we were spinning out our lines, walking on the wire,
Hand in hand went music and the rhyme.
The Captain and the Kid stepping in the ring,
From here on sonny, it's a long and lonely climb.'

As is the case with many musical superstars, in time Elton's music became a little less soulful and a bit more schmaltzy. But we loved him just the same. However popular Elton's music became with the fans, none of his tunes was as well-liked as the theme tune to a 1962 BBC TV drama about Liverpool policemen. *Z-Cars* was the then Watford manager Bill McGarry's favourite show and at the start of the 1963/64 season the club chose the music to be played as the team ran on to the pitch. It became something of a lucky charm as it coincided with the start of the club's longest unbeaten home run in its history – 27 games. Although Ken Furphy abandoned it in 1966, when Graham Taylor arrived at Watford he asked Oliver Phillips if there was any tune from the past that might be suitable to play before the home games.

'I mentioned *Z-Cars* and the unbeaten home record and it was played throughout the entire Taylor era and on into the Glenn Roeder era too until the commercial manager thought it needed updating,' Phillips explained.

The club went through several periods when the powers that be assumed the supporters were attending some Ibiza-influenced outdoor rave rather than a football match, and wanted to hear loud monotonous bass-driven music rather than enjoy a nice chat with their mates or have a quick look at the programme in peace. The club did go to the other extreme when they started playing Coldplay's 'Yellow' for a spell, but that tended to send everyone to sleep. A similar slow-paced song was also used when the theme tune from the film *Chariots of Fire*, by Greek composer Vangelis, was introduced. This was a fine tune but about as slow as you could get. In the film I believe it accompanies a scene of the athletes running in slow motion on a beach. When my pals and I were sitting in the Rookery, we would instinctively move in slow motion to the music, rather like the players under Gianluca 'we are down to the bare bones' Vialli used to do.

Of the faster-paced tunes that were played, my favourite was 'Tubthumping' by Burnley's finest, Chumbawamba. For your average football fan, this song scored on all fronts. It had a simple beat combined with a raucous 'you can all join in' chorus of 'I get knocked down but I get up again, they aren't ever gonna keep me down', which fans empathised with. I liked it and still do. It was the perfect pre-match tune: happy, easy to sing and positive. I do hope they play it regularly at Turf Moor. In the late 70s and early 80s, Elvis Costello's 'Oliver's Army' was tried but never really worked. I imagined it could easily incite any of the more temperamental and aggressive fans to get involved in some pre-match fisticuffs.

Almost 20 years after he first took me to see Watford, I finally persuaded Dad to visit Vicarage Road again on Saturday, 9 March 1981. I had been trying for several years to get him to come to a home game with me, but he always refused, citing football violence, unsavoury language and loutish behaviour as the reasons. I told him that Watford was now a friendly family club and there would be no trouble. He was still unsure but, as it was his birthday, he relented and we made our way to watch the game against Queen's Park Rangers. Twenty minutes before kick-off we were standing in my usual spot, about three-quarters of the way back behind the goal at the Vicarage Road end, when a well-built menacing-looking man in his mid-thirties came and stood directly behind us. I'd never seen him before and paid no attention to him until, just before kick-off, 'Oliver's Army' was played on the PA. Cue the newcomer (the burly bloke, not my dad) to join in and sing an ear-damaging duet with Elvis, not so much singing as screaming 'We could be in Palestine!' at the top of his voice in my dad's left earhole. 'Overrun by a Chinese line, with the boys from the Mersey and the Thames and the Tyne.' He knew all the words.

By now Dad was wincing and shuffling from foot to foot, 'resembling a man in the early stages of the hully-gully', as Clive James once described Eddie Waring on *It's A Knockout*. I thought about asking the man if he did requests and could sing 'Shipbuilding' for us, but decided against it. Instead Dad and I moved to an alternative, quieter and less threatening spot some yards away. Watford went on to win the game 4-0 with goals from Les Taylor, Luther Blissett, Ross Jenkins and an own goal. In many ways I was the one who scored an own goal and that was the last time Dad saw a Watford game. I do remember the away game with QPR the following season. It ended in a goalless draw, but before the game started I asked one of the policemen outside the ground, 'Which is the away supporters' end?' He pointed to his left, saying: 'Go down there, mate. The other end's where all the fuckin' QPR Rangers supporters go.' From that day on, I have always referred to that club as QPR Rangers …

CHAPTER 10

Behind the Scenes

IN THE modern game, most supporters tend to concentrate on the star players and successful managers of their chosen teams. Hardly surprising, I suppose, as both are often treated as celebrities and superstars. This increase in attention, plus the money at stake, has meant that some of the backroom staff, so important in the day-to-day running of any football club, get forgotten. Back in the 60s and early 70s, before Graham Taylor arrived and established Watford as a family club, there were a bunch of individuals behind the scenes that made the club tick. I've picked out a few of them.

Les Simmons

I know this may sound daft to any reader under the age of 30, but there was a time when football was played on real grass and the only equipment used to maintain the playing surface was a mower, some chalk to mark the lines, heaps of sand to soak up the water, heaps of hay to keep off the frost, and Les Simmons with his fork to help drain the pitch at half-time.

Groundsman Les was a one-man maintenance machine and one of the great characters of the club. For over 50 years he looked after the pitch seven days a week, often arriving to start his work at 6am, always with a smile on his face and a joke ready on the tip of his tongue. His dedication to the club was absolute.

A day or so before the home game against Rotherham United, scheduled for Saturday, 8 February 1969, the club announced that they were to lay several tons of hay on the pitch on the Friday afternoon and evening to protect it against the severe overnight frost that was forecast. As a result, an SOS was put out for as many fans as possible to turn up at the ground on Saturday morning to help Les and his team clear the pitch. I duly volunteered and joined about 200 hardy souls in doing my bit. It was to prove well worth it; not only did we win 5-1 – with a rare brace from Walter Lees and singles from Barry Endean, Tom Walley and Dixie Hale – but the match, just about the only one in the country to survive the weather, was also later televised on *Match of the Day*.

For many supporters, Les, and his band of assistants, would provide the half-time entertainment at home games, trudging on to the pitch armed with a fork to help drain the pitch and give it some air. He would also stay on after many winter evening games, repairing any damaged turf before the overnight frost set in. He was also very knowledgeable about the club, happy to talk about former managers, players and board members with anyone who wanted to listen. He had a marvellous sense of humour and always managed a cheery word for everyone.

Les, who passed away in December 2009, was granted a testimonial game against Arsenal in May 1997. In his programme notes for the game, Graham Taylor paid tribute to him: 'The pace of turf technology has speeded up considerably in recent years and the maintenance of the playing surface is increasingly being contracted out to specialist firms. That is now the case at Watford. In many ways that makes Les's achievements over the last half-century all the more astonishing. The fact that we actually played football on "his" pitch is also astonishing, as he guarded the playing surface jealously.

'Indeed, many are the times when Les's dulcet tones could be heard ringing around the stadium on non-matchdays – "Get off my f****** pitch", and we did, chairman, directors, manager, players, staff members – we all respected Les. So occasionally it used to give me a perverse pleasure on a muddy December afternoon to watch a slide tackle go in and four feet of turf come slicing off the surface. I'd turn to look at Les in the tunnel, hoping I could send him a knowing grin. But again he used to thwart me, because he couldn't look back – he was holding his head in his hands. I'm sure if you could have said "Get off my f****** pitch" on a matchday he would have done. But I would go as far as to say that Les influenced the outcome of matches. When we played with two wingers and needed to keep the game flowing down the flanks, having a surface that gave the likes of Barnes and Callaghan the ability to run confidently with the ball was vital to our success.'

Molly Rush

Another person who worked hard behind the scenes in the old days of the 60s and 70s was the club's official tea lady, Molly Rush. Molly used to make endless cups of tea every day for the manager, board members, players and anyone else who wanted one. She would also prepare food and snacks for the board and any guests visiting the club. And that's not all; she washed the players' match-day and training kit, and her favourite manager was Bill McGarry because he was the first person to buy her a club washing machine!

Tom Walley

You hear Tom Walley before you see him. That booming Welsh voice, a mix of sergeant major and Dylan Thomas, would ring out around Woodside Sports Centre on a Saturday morning in the early 1980s, encouraging and admonishing the youth-team players in equal measure. 'Lukas Louka, what are you doing, boy? Don't mess around with the ball. Use it!' The passion was there for everyone to see and hear. And talking of passion, there's a story concerning an on-field encounter between Tom and Luton's Bruce Rioch at Kenilworth Road in April 1969, which led to both players being sent off. The 'discussions' between them continued as they made their way to their respective dressing rooms. By the time Tom got to the away team's door he was in a rage and, with one almighty kick from his trusty left foot, the door flew off its hinges and landed on the floor.

Caernarfon-born Tom had two spells at the club as a player, the first between 1967 and 1971 and the second between 1976 and 1978. Always totally committed, this hard-working, hard-tackling midfielder with a tremendous left-foot shot always gave 100 per cent, something he was to continue to do when, coming to the end of his playing career at Watford, Graham Taylor asked him if he was interested in running the youth team.

'My knee had given up and I had been offered a job at Leyton Orient and I was going to take it. Graham said, "Would you like to come on the staff and do the youth?" I said yes, but I have to go back up home and talk to the missus because if I'm going to do it and be successful it's a 24-hour-a-day mission. So we had a chat and sorted it out. Graham said, "Okay, off you go, it's your job. Get on with it." Graham is a clever man, make no mistake. We got on well together but he was the gaffer and he kept an eye on things and also coached them a bit.'

Tom's predecessor, Dave Butler, already had two promising lads – Kenny Jackett and Nigel Callaghan – but training facilities were limited at that time. 'We went up the gym at the YMCA and had Cassiobury Park in the summer, then we had the car park where the ticket office is now. We improved the facilities a bit. Dennis Gibbs was a huge help. We then went up to Woodside.' Tom's dedication was already evident: 'I went hunting 24 hours a day. Watching games, watching players. Talking to parents. I was up at Swansea one Saturday morning. John Toshack, who was at Swansea then, was there. "What are you doing here?" Same as you, I want players. After half an hour I'd sneak away. I'd got the phone numbers I wanted.'

From the start Tom was honest with the parents, never building up their or their son's hopes. 'I'd say, "Your boy has a chance if he comes to us. We'll work on him. We'll put the hours in and make him a player. I can't guarantee you nothing but he will work hard and he'll learn and we'll give him every chance we can."' Gradually Tom built up a nucleus of players. 'I went to Cheshunt and I picked Steve Terry up there. I was doing all the scouting. I was going here, there and everywhere.

We had Bradley Walsh, the comedian, but he wasn't quite good enough for us. I had 24 kids to start with and I only .kept three – the goalkeeper, Cally and Jackett - so we had to build up and go and get players.

'Today you've got children of seven in clubs and their old man or their old lady thinks that's it, they're going to play for Man United. I don't agree with it. It's only an opinion but a boy of seven, he doesn't know what day of the week it is. He just wants to play about, have fun. He's not a footballer but they make 'em think they're footballers. They're not. It's too soon. There should be a network of small clubs, local clubs all playing kids' football, a big network of clubs that you keep an eye on. You don't need a boy of ten signing for a club. It's daft.'

These were the days before smaller players like Lionel Messi and Andrés Iniesta were chosen for their talent, technique and ability rather than size. Tom was once told he might not make the grade. 'I went to Sheffield Wednesday when I was 14 and the coach came onto the pitch and said to me, "Yeah, you've got ability but you're too small, be a jockey." Three-and-a-half years later I am playing for Arsenal against their first team just after Christmas when I came on as a sub, then played the full game the following day. You don't make a decision until you have to.'

Tom realised the importance of instilling a winning mentality into the boys at an early age. 'I wanted to win, course I did, but I wanted the players to win too. If you're going to be in the first team you got to be better than the rest in the youth team. I was looking for talent. I hunted, and got Jimmy Gilligan, Steve Terry, Charlie Palmer and Wally Sterling in. Paul Merson was training with us and one night he didn't come. Anyway, Merson had gone to Arsenal, and his old mum had got a brand-new washing machine out of it. We never paid for players but we didn't have a chance to offer her a washing machine! We never paid, we weren't at it. That was the way we went, but I might have offered her a washing machine for him!'

There were certain things Tom was looking for in a player: 'You look at the boy and look at what he's got. The main thing is a bit of technique, is he quick, has he got a bit of know-how, can he pull away from people. I can give him a few things, but I looked for the little basics. If he had that at 13, 14, I'd say okay, boy, you come in and I'll have a go with you. I'd find out about the mental side too. I'd find out about the attitude quickly. I didn't have a good attitude when I was young. I didn't like to run because I wasn't good at it, so I started to run. I was doing four-and-a-half-minute miles and I started to get fit. I told them that fitness levels are the easy things to get. That's just work. You work and you work and you work. Easy. Anyone can do that. But they have to be fit to make the most of what they have.

'Then you look at the technique and improve what they've got. Have they got a bit of vision? Can they pass the ball? Can they think about the game? Have they got a bit of quickness about them? That was what coaching was about. We worked hard with them.' And Tom also taught them the meaning of discipline. 'Football is a game but it's not a joke. You can have a laugh at the right time but you got to stay in the game and that takes work. I'd test them. You've got to get on to them, see if they come back at you. I used to really moan at them to see what their reactions would be. I'd pull them in and say, "Now son, I'm going to tell you how you've gone on."

'I used to ring them up at home on a Friday night. If they were out, as 17, 18-year-old boys, if they were late home they'd hear all about it from me. I used to say to their parents and their landladies you work with me, not with them. If they're out, I need to know. If I ring at 10pm and they're there, I'm happy, but I want to speak to them. You work with me now. If they were out, I'd give them one warning, then second time, out. No messing. You can't play about with it. Once you start playing about you start losing your chance. You've got to look after the body. You've got to be fit, you've got to give yourself a chance if you want to be a professional footballer. Eat right, don't drink, keep fit all year.' Eventually Tom's lads had to be good enough for the first team. 'We didn't have a load of money to buy half a new team every season, we had to bring these boys through. As we went on we had to change it. Remember, we were in the Fourth Division when we started. They needed to be big, strong with good skill, but I looked for a bit extra. Can they move the ball with pace? Can they move people about? After a few years we knew they had to be good enough for the Second Division now, then the First Division.

'We'd match them up with the first team, wingers, crossing into the box. We had a way of playing and it was the same throughout the club. My lads had to fit in with the reserves and they had to fit in with the top man's team.'

Again Tom emphasises the importance of discipline. 'I'd been disciplined the right way. All my players, we used to have laughs but if they messed me about they would know about it, but we'd have a crack. I used to love my kids in any case, even when I was shouting at 'em. It was a full-time job, every day. Training the young ones on Monday and Thursday nights, watching games every spare minute. I used to travel all over the shop on my own. My wife used to wash the kit and make the food.'

And Tom needed to be clever, one step ahead of the other scouts: 'Sometimes I'd go with Jimmy Howard because there'd be other scouts there so I'd have someone go over and get the number because if I went over it would give the other scouts some leads on who I was interested in. I'd go home and ring up his mam. I'd always try to ring first. She said, "You're the first one to ring, you can have him." Lads who lived away I'd go and pick up. I used to go and pick up Jimmy Gilligan from Stevenage. I used to go down to Bristol on a Friday to pick up someone else. We'd play on Saturday morning and then I'd drive him back. People talk about work! It was work and it was long, long days. Often up before it was light and not home till after midnight but it was work I loved doing.'

Tom reckoned the hardest part of the job was when he had to let a player go. 'Every now and then they didn't have that little bit extra. You knew you were breaking his heart but you had to do it. I'd say, "There's more clubs than Watford. You go and prove me wrong, son." One or two did but I was a pretty good judge. If I let one go I didn't think they had it. But I wouldn't change my life, I had a great time. Wouldn't change a thing.'

Nigel Callaghan was one player he remembered with affection. 'He was a good boy. He was really interesting. He wanted to be with me all the time. He wanted to come down and do coaching with me when he was in the first team and Graham said, "He can't come with you all the time." But he just liked to hang about with us.

'We could have signed Mark Hughes for £50,000 before he went to Man United. Nearly let Iwan Roberts go to Man

United but we got him. As we went through the divisions, we had more finance and better facilities. We had Stanmore then so there was a good place to train. Graham lived down the road from me and he came round here of a night one day and he says, "Now Tom, what do you reckon, I've had an offer for Luther for a million pounds, what do you reckon?" I said, "Take it." When Graham came in, he spoke to me. First day I was youth coach he asked me, "What do you think you have here?" I said there's some good players who ain't been worked on. There's Luther Blissett, who was supposed to go with my brother to Crystal Palace because they were going to release him. I said, "Don't release, he's different gears, eh? He just needs work." Same with Ross Jenkins. Lovely footballer. But they needed work. They needed to learn the runs, work on finishing off the crosses. But they were giving up on 'em.'

What the players said:

Two members of the Hornets' 1982 FA Youth Cup-winning side, Neil Price and David Johnson, have paid tribute to the coaching of Tom Walley in masterminding a dramatic win over a stellar Manchester United side that included Mark Hughes, Norman Whiteside and Clayton Blackmore. The Hornets lifted the cup following a thrilling 7-6 aggregate win over the Red Devils, a victory clinched with a 4-4 draw at Vicarage Road in front of more than 8,000 fans. A 103rd-minute header from Jimmy Gilligan sealed the result and left-back Neil Price attributes the win to the coaching and man-management of Walley.

'I don't think there has been a better youth coach in this country,' said Price, who ended up playing in the FA Cup for the Hornets two years after the FA Youth Cup Final win.

'People talk about Eric Harrison at United and the Class of '92, but Tom did it with group after group and won the Youth Cup at other clubs too and is loved at Arsenal and Millwall. He got players from nowhere and made them into top players. His first lot were Kenny Jackett, Nigel Gibbs and Steve Terry and then we had a group after that and another group after that. We had a really strong youth team and yet you were always looking over your shoulder as there were people he had got in and coached ready to take your place.'

Johnson played on the left wing in both games against United and scored three goals in the run to the final. 'Tom Walley was so underrated as a coach,' he said. 'He was like a sergeant major and didn't take any nonsense but he never bore a grudge – he just told you how it was. He had total belief in you as a player and was one of the best youth coaches ever in this country. A lot of players have got him to thank for their careers. He didn't just make you professional footballers, he made you responsible young men. A lot of his teachings I have passed down to my kids. He was years ahead of his time.'

Ron Rollitt

When I was younger and starting to support the club, I thought club secretary Ron Rollitt must have been a workaholic. This was because for a long time the only photo used in the club programme was one of him sitting at his desk with a telephone stuck to his right ear. Here's Oliver Phillips's account of Ron's time at Watford:

'Ron joined Watford FC in 1955 and served under successive chairmen in T. Rigby Taylor, Jim Bonser and lastly Elton John, during a 26-year spell at the heart of Vicarage Road. Ironically he joined the club on April Fool's Day and had a sign on his desk that encapsulated his philosophical view of the job: "You don't have to be mad to work here but it certainly helps."

'In 1955, Watford were in Division Three South, soon to become founder members of Division Four when the Football League was reorganised, and their status was reflected by stringent financial policies. For many years, Ron was responsible for the wages, boardroom reports and minutes, fielding press inquiries, dealing with members of the public who called in on sundry issues and he was also responsible for ticket sales and organising the club programme.

'He had a secretary who worked mornings-only and with so many facets to his job, including dealing with players' complaints about leaking taps or other such problems experienced in the dozen or so club houses, it is a wonder he retained his sanity. When I remarked on that fact one day after a myriad of interruptions as we attempted to conclude our weekly interview update, he just pointed to the sign on his desk with a smile.

'Yet despite the hectic, chaotic nature of the job, he remained polite, helpful and always had time whenever someone looked to him for help, advice or an opinion. He was among the nicest people one could wish to meet and, for my part, I was extremely grateful that he was there when I cut my teeth in local journalism and covering Watford. Ron smoothed the way with a kindly: "Yes, young man. What can I do for you?"

'In the early 1970s, he asked me if I had any use for a football cartoon, submitted for the programme. "We have used one but can't make a habit of it," he explained. I took the cartoon, used it and the Terry Challis cartoon became a key part of the *Watford Observer* coverage. He was also the Voice of Watford, in that it was his tones that were heard on the Tannoy system announcing team changes, half-time scores, dedications and on occasions his angry instructions to fans: "Get off the pitch. Get off THAT pitch."

'Other fans may recall when pick-pocketing seemed to be the rage in the late 1950s, Ron warned the crowd stating, "Make sure the hand in your pocket is your own." During his years at the administrative helm, he saw the Cliff Holton-inspired promotion and FA Cup run (1960), promotion to the second tier for the first time in the club's history (1969) and was at the door to welcome an inquisitive pop star and Watford fan, Elton John. Among his treasured possessions was a telegram from the star, congratulating him on 25 years of service for the club.

'In the 1970s, Ron was given the title general manager but in effect he had undertaken those duties for many years, but the man who used to say as a parting remark, "Press on reward-less", appreciated the recognition. However, following the arrival of Graham Taylor, assistant manager Bertie Mee and chief executive Eddie Plumley, Ron became more of a backroom figure and it was decided his services were no longer needed.

'Negotiations took place and the plainly disappointed former secretary announced he was taking early retirement at the age of 58. A year later, Watford gained promotion to the top flight – Premiership as it is now. Within a very short time Ron joined the *Watford Observer* on the auditing side and remained a fondly remembered, genial colleague for many years, working part-time after his retirement. Graham Taylor: 'Ron was an excellent "behind the scenes" man who helped me settle into Watford FC in my first two years as manager. The role he played for the club over a long period of time should never be underestimated.'

Eddie Plumley

The circumstances surrounding how Eddie Plumley joined the club in 1978 are a significant pointer as to how the club were 'thinking big' in their plans for the future. 'How Elton John, Graham Taylor and the board were building a football club, not just a football team,' as Lionel Birnie put it in *Enjoy the Game,* his absorbing account of Watford's rise to the top. 'As the players took the club from the Fourth Division to the First in five years the club had to keep up. The ramshackle old stadium needed a lot of work and I knew that Eddie Plumley, who joined the club in 1978, would be able to talk about what it was like building up the club.'

Here's Eddie's take on how he joined the bandwagon: 'I was general secretary at Coventry City and Watford advertised for an executive manager. I hadn't seen the advert, and I hadn't a clue what an executive manager was. I was chairman of the secretaries and managers association, which was the collection of football club secretaries, chief executives and senior management. Watford's assistant manager Bertie Mee was in the association and he came to see me that November time when they were already making a good fist of getting out of Division Four. He came to ask my opinion.

'They wanted someone to run the administrative side. They had Ron Rollitt as company secretary but they wanted an executive manager to take on a senior role working with the board, the chairman, the manager. I said I didn't like the title. I wasn't sure they'd get the right person with that title. Bertie asked me if I could recommend someone. I don't think they were struggling to fill the post, I think they were struggling to find the right person. He said, "We've had over a hundred applications, but there's nothing that hits us between the eyes." I said well, give me time to think about it. A little later, Bertie came up to a reserve game at Coventry one afternoon to talk to me about it again. I gave him a couple of names and he shook his head. He said: "Well, what about yourself?"

'I said well, hang on a minute, I am general secretary of a First Division club. Why would I want to do that? He said, "At least come and meet Elton. You know Graham. Come and talk. You might be interested." I met up with Elton. He knew of me, but he didn't know me. After some long talks I could see they were going to go places, no question about it. He was a winner and he was determined to put in place a group of people to get Watford to the First Division. There was no hiding their ambition – they wanted to be successful. You could tell that Elton, Graham and Bertie were looking for the last piece in the jigsaw. That may sound a bit big-headed and I don't mean that at all, but they wanted to get on with matters on the pitch and they needed someone to knit everything else together, try to improve the stadium, build the club up.

'The job was to look after everything on the administrative side and legal side, and to work for Graham Taylor, who was called general manager. It was virtually everything but the football, but I had played professionally so I had the knowledge of a football club and knew how it worked. I'd done all the jobs so if it was the maintenance man, or the ticket office girl, or a player coming in, I could deal with it. I suppose I was quite a good guy to recruit in that sense because I knew how all aspects of a football club should work.

'I got on with things as they came up. There was a lot to do and it was a full-time job and a half at times but I remember when I was at Coventry the stand had burned down and I had to rebuild that in the time I was there. I had a lot of admiration for what Jimmy Hill did. He had a phrase, "If you give a busy man a job, he'll do it," and that's how I saw myself. I was never still. When I got to Watford in the April there was no question about it, they were going to go up into the Third Division. The next year they went into the Second Division, so from my point of view I'd been in all four divisions in under two years.'

CHAPTER 11

On the Road

MY FIRST away game was with Laurie for a midweek League Cup encounter at Bournemouth in August 1967, whilst on holiday at my grandparents' in nearby Highcliffe.

My mum's parents, Nancy and Fred, lived in a small bungalow with an old air-raid shelter at the bottom of the garden that was used to store food, as it was cool. These were the days when a fridge was a luxury. Fred would often call out to his wife: 'I'm going down the doins Nance.' We spent summer holidays there, where days were spent on the beach and evenings consisted of playing games like snakes and ladders and Kan-You-Go. Fred would say: 'Paul, can you go? I should coco!' Laurie spent a good deal of time train-spotting too.

The following year I experienced my first local derby when I caught the 321 bus to visit Luton's Kenilworth Road ground. It was a lovely trip on an August evening for a League Cup tie. I had been used to travelling with my mum to St Albans as a little boy – particularly to visit Wrens sports and toy shop on Holywell Hill – but venturing any further north was unheard of. As soon as we trundled through the leafy landscape that was Harpenden, I thought we were going to end up in some kind of idyllic country retreat, complete with a village green, little shops that sold postcards and a pub with a cricket pitch opposite.

Alas, it was not to be. By the time we arrived at Luton town centre, we were greeted by most of the Bedfordshire Constabulary, a few on horses and many with large dogs. Some of them were kind enough to walk with us to the ground and managed not to join in with all the jolly songs the Luton fans were singing to us: 'We hate Watford, we hate Watford' and 'You're gonna get your f****** heads kicked in', which I presume they were singing to us and not the boys in blue. Mind you, they were working themselves into such a frenzy that they would probably have given the SAS a good run for their money. When we arrived at the ground I was shocked to find it was in an even worse state than 'The Vic'. Nevertheless it didn't stop 25,000 fans from cramming into the place to see Luton win 3-0. Then it was back to the bus stop home, thankfully once again accompanied by our newly acquired policemen chums.

The first long-distance away match I went to was too far to get to in a car. Anyway, I don't think Dad would have been too pleased with me borrowing his Ford Escort GT and allowing me to drive up to Manchester as a 13-year-old! So instead Alan Patterson and I caught the 321 bus for the first part of our journey. At the time it seemed such a simple thing to do, but looking back it does seem quite an adventurous journey to undertake at such a young age. We walked to the bus stop early on that Saturday morning of 25 January 1969 to catch the bus to Watford Junction on the first stage of our trip. Next we'd catch a 'soccer special' train to Manchester to watch Watford play the recently crowned European champions Manchester United in the fourth round of the FA Cup. I travelled sporting a new Watford scarf plus my trusty wooden rattle for extra good luck. Mum had packed lunch for me and we had a cup of tea and a snack on the train. The train trip took a little over two hours to reach Manchester Piccadilly station and we alighted at around 12.30. In years to come, that would have given us plenty of time to sample a couple of beers and a pie in a local pub, but back then we settled for a sedate stroll to the ground instead. What could possibly go wrong?

We had only been walking for about five minutes when I was attacked by three or four local louts, one of whom kicked me in the groin and ran off with my scarf. As I was getting to my feet I noticed two bigger lads were chasing after my assailants and, thinking they were Watford fans, I looked forward to getting my prized scarf back. One of the lads had my scarf in his hand and said: 'Here you go, we're not all hooligans, you know.' He motioned as if to give me the scarf back before snatching it away again and running off laughing. This was to be my first introduction to northern humour and I wasn't laughing – aching but not laughing. No matter, I was relatively unhurt and we walked the three and a half miles to the ground with no further problems. Arriving at the ground we looked around the impressive stadium that was quite unlike the tired and tatty Vicarage Road ground that I was used to. By comparison this looked like a huge spacecraft. When we got inside we were soon joined by 63,496 other spectators. That was when the sheer size of the occasion really hit home. Of course the game, along with the Watford performance, which I will describe later, bore no mark of fear or intimidation and in years to come Old Trafford proved to be a happy hunting ground.

By the time I was 14 I had acquired the taste for part-time employment and the money that went with it. As well as an evening paper round, I was also working weekend and evening shifts at the local Esso garage down the road. I enjoyed both, although the work at the garage could be tough. Maureen was my boss, but the garage was run by two brothers – Bob and George Cox. On my first visit Bob smiled and was friendly, and George looked as happy as a turkey at Christmas, and even had a straggly neck to match. Maureen was known to everyone as 'blondie'. This was ten years before Debbie Harry arrived on the pop scene. But despite being a hard taskmaster, Maureen had a heart of gold. It's true she never allowed me to take a break – forever keeping me busy serving the customers, replenishing the shelves and cleaning the pumps – but we enjoyed a good laugh, poking fun at the customers, and Bob and George too once they went home at 6pm.

My paper round was more relaxed and involved me cycling round to pick up about 40 copies of the *Evening Echo* from Mrs Murphy's house in Jordan's Way, Bricket Wood, and delivering them to houses close by. Saturdays were trickier as I had to collect the weekly cash of three shillings and thruppence, or as one ancient customer used to say in a voice similar to Henry Crun in *The Goon Show* as soon as he opened his front door, 'Three and three?' I had my own *Evening Echo* delivery bag, which I slung over my shoulder. I should think the whole round took under an hour to complete and, although I didn't realise it at the time, it was a doddle.

My next job was far harder work, but it paid well. I joined forces with my pal Alan Patterson and we formed a brief but profitable partnership providing a local window-cleaning service, working for five or six hours on Saturday mornings and early afternoons. We had the basic equipment of bucket, soap, sponge and squeegie, and we also splashed out on a dash of vinegar to prevent smears. The one thing we didn't have was a ladder. This wasn't as big a problem as it sounds. Bricket Wood was, as it is now, a village containing mainly bungalows, which for us ladderless lads was perfect. By working together we could complete a bungalow in about 20 minutes. On a good day we often managed to make as much as £15 each, equivalent to £150 today. We worked hard and, apart from one incident, it was trouble and argument-free. Mum's friend, Dina Buckingham, lived up the road in one of the few modern townhouses in the village. Mum must have mentioned our new business venture to her, as we soon had an appointment to clean her windows. We decided it was best not to tell her we didn't possess a ladder and strolled round there that week at the end of our round.

Once we had finished the lower windows, I made the decision to ask Dina's rather disagreeable husband, Den, if we could borrow his ladder. Being a grumpy old sod he, quite understandably, questioned our professionalism, intelligence, cheek, sanity, etc., as he lugged his extendable ladder out of the garage. I'm sure there were a few expletives thrown in too, but he kept them to himself, muttering under his breath. We completed the top windows rather speedily, collected our money and scarpered sharpish. We didn't have the courage to return a fortnight later and, unsurprisingly, were never invited back. Our window-cleaning days lasted for a couple of years, which meant visits to Vicarage Road were restricted to the occasional midweek match with Mrs Lane or Laurie.

After Ken Furphy left for Blackburn Rovers in 1971 I felt disappointed. The George Kirby and Mike Keen years that followed were difficult but I, along with many fans, stuck it out. After all, we were used to struggling; a realistic bunch, brought up by parents and friends who recognised that Watford were a small-town club and used to life in the bottom two divisions. It didn't mean we loved the club less. If anything, being the underdog meant the opposite – we could look forward to all those epic cup ties where, with a bit of luck, we could upset the big boys.

This stoicism was in many ways nurtured by Jim Bonser. Supporters knew he wasn't particularly ambitious and also very careful with his money, but in those days he wasn't alone. There were a number of chairmen with a similar philosophy. Bob Lord at Burnley and Albert Alexander at Manchester City were two examples. There is an amusing tale featuring the latter's pre-match motivational speech before the 1969 FA Cup semi-final against Everton at Villa Park. This was a golden era for the club and, under the management team of Joe Mercer and Malcolm Allison, they had won the league title the previous season. Manchester City's players were buzzing as Francis Lee explains: 'Albert Alexander made a tear-jerking speech ahead of the game. The dressing room was reeking of embrocation when Joe suddenly said, "Quiet boys, the chairman would like a few words with you." Albert, bless him, came in and said: "It's very good to be here. Good luck to everybody and if we win, we can get to Wembley. Then we'll get plenty of money and win in front of a big crowd and then we can buy some new better players!" You can imagine how well that went down!' It worked though – a Tommy Booth goal earned City a 1-0 win and a place against Leicester in the final.

Watford's fortunes were also about to improve. After Jim Bonser eventually resigned in 1976, Elton John took over as chairman. One of his first jobs was to look for a new manager, and the leading candidate was Bobby Moore. Yes, Elton's first choice for Watford manager was the former England captain and World Cup winner who had recently retired from playing for Fulham and expressed an interest in management. The board – and in particular Muir Stratford and Geoff Smith – were not so sure, believing the club needed someone more used to life in the lower leagues. They were impressed by Lincoln City, who had twice beaten Watford the previous season on their way to the Fourth Division title. More importantly, they had met their manager Graham Taylor after the game at Vicarage Road and Stratford remembered it well: 'You don't have to spend very long with people to get a feel for them, and I think both Geoff and I were immediately impressed.' Taylor talked quickly but clearly with a passion that was hard to resist.

Elton respected their views and sought advice from the then England manager Don Revie, who told him: 'Graham Taylor at Lincoln City is the man you want.' When Revie phoned Taylor to ask him if he was under contract at Lincoln, Taylor told him he was. When he found out Watford's chairman was interested in him, he was taken aback and felt a little disappointed. 'Lincoln were in the Third Division and Watford were a division lower, what would I want to go there for?' he asked. Taylor also didn't know who Elton John was. Elton went back to his original choice and met with Moore in London for lunch. After the meeting they shook hands and Moore, believing the deal was done, awaited the final details, before contacting his good friend Jeff Powell, the well-known football journalist on the *Daily Mail,* who ran the story the next day.

Stratford and Smith were worried and contacted Elton immediately. Relieved to discover the deal with Moore hadn't been signed, they persuaded Elton that Taylor was the best man for Watford. This, plus the fact that Revie had already said much the same thing, swayed the new chairman, and he phoned Taylor requesting a meeting at his Windsor home. 'It was like entering a different world,' Taylor recalled. 'He offered me a five-year contract worth four and a half times more than I was getting at Lincoln.' But it wasn't just the money that counted for Taylor. He asked Elton what he expected to achieve at a club that had spent only three years in the second tier of English football and the rest of the time in the lower divisions. Elton's reply was: 'I'd like to get into Europe.' Taylor thought he was joking or mad, or possibly both, so he asked him what he thought it might cost to achieve this. Elton didn't know and asked Taylor for a figure. 'I don't think you'll have much change out of a million pounds.' 'Right, we'll give it a go,' was the reply. Taylor, noticing the steely look in Elton's eyes, thought, 'That'll do for me.'

This was the summer of 1977 and most of the country was in party mood, having already tasted some musical success when Lynsey de Paul and Mike Moran finished second in the Eurovision Song Contest with their cheeky little tune, 'Rock Bottom'. More celebrations would follow with the Royal Silver Jubilee and Virginia Wade's rather mundane victory over the bulky Betty Stöve in the Women's Singles Final at

Wimbledon. Unbeknown to us, there would be good times on the way for Watford Football Club too.

Like Elton, I knew nothing about Graham Taylor. However, it didn't take too long to notice a difference in how we played the game and who was playing it. Just a week or so after Dan Maskell had been saying, 'Oh I say, well played Virginia, well played indeed!' Graham Taylor would be putting the Watford players through a somewhat more vigorous physical test than jolly old Virginia was used to. The Watford squad had never experienced anything quite like pre-season training that July. The new boss had already made his mark by getting rid of the cinder greyhound track running round the pitch, saying to Elton: 'It's either the dogs or me.' He then held one-to-one meetings with all the playing staff to gauge their personalities and explain what their football life would be like under his management, preparing them for the new regime. He was going to run the club his way and, for the next few weeks, the players were just going to run. They'd sprint round the pitch where the dogs used to run, they'd run up and down the Vicarage Road terrace. There were ten-mile cross-country runs through Cassiobury Park and Whippendell Woods, 400-metre sprints one after another, gym work at the YMCA, and aerobic sessions too. It was relentless, with two training sessions a day, and a bit of ball work – crossing and shooting – thrown in for good measure.

The players needed to be super-fit if they were going to play Taylor's long-ball, high-powered and pressing style of football. And that meant playing full-on for 90 minutes. The full-backs would be encouraged to attack at every opportunity, and all the players would look for the forward pass. Taylor also liked to play with a big target man up front, which proved to be good news for Ross Jenkins, whose game gradually blossomed under Taylor's tutelage. He learnt how to hold the ball up, how to make the right runs and, vitally, how to finish. Taylor took an immediate shine to another young striker who was starting out on his Watford journey. Luther Blissett was to learn the game along with Jenkins, and the duo soon formed a formidable and fruitful partnership.

After establishing that most of the squad were behind him, Taylor was ready to make a couple of signings. Sam Ellis arrived that July for £6,000. At almost 32, Ellis was Taylor's captain at Lincoln – as hard physically and mentally as Taylor – and a true leader. He started at the top, making his debut for Sheffield Wednesday as a 19-year-old in the 1966 FA Cup Final against Everton at Wembley. Ellis went on to manage Blackpool and Bury before becoming Peter Reid's assistant at Manchester City. He later became Lincoln's manager in 1994.

A few hours later, centre-half Ian Bolton arrived for £12,000 from Notts County. It was a bargain price because Bolton had a long-term back problem. Even so, this elegant and deceptively quick player would go on to make more than 200 appearances, either in defence or midfield, chipping in with 28 goals. Taylor was later to describe Bolton as his best-ever signing. When reading former Notts County midfielder David McVay's highly entertaining and amusing account of life in the lower leagues during the 1970s – *Steak Diana Ross* – I was surprised to learn that Bolton was not only a chain-smoker but also the quickest player on County's books.

Watford got off to a good start and, following a League Cup tie at West Bromwich Albion at the end of October, signed another player who was to have a big influence on the club – Dennis Booth. Again a former colleague of Taylor's at Lincoln, Booth was an all-action, tough-tackling midfielder who shared Taylor's work ethic on the pitch. Like Ellis and Bolton, he was also an important influence off it. Ellis and Booth knew Taylor well and they transformed the dressing room. Skipper Ellis in particular was an intelligent, straight-talking man who wasn't afraid to say his piece, but he did so in a positive way that galvanised the squad.

At around the same time that the players were learning a new way to play, I was learning how to drive a motor car. Unfortunately, I wasn't as quick a learner as Ross and Luther, and my lessons with Ernie Entwistle were to become a weekly affair after I failed my test the first time. I must say, however, that the elements were against me on that rainy winter's day when I arrived in Watford to take my initial test. Things started encouragingly enough, when I discovered I would be driving a Mini almost identical to Ernie's model, which I had been driving around Bricket Wood, St Albans and Watford for months. But it all started to go wrong before I'd even made it to the car. The rain was lashing down and the dark clouds made it feel like dusk, even though it was mid-morning. If I'd have been playing cricket, the umpire's light meter would have gone haywire and we'd have been enjoying an early lunch and a cup of tea. No such luck. The instructor, glancing at his clipboard, uttered those fated few words: 'Now, Mr Bishop, can you please tell me the registration number of that car over there?' I peered hopelessly through the soaked lenses of my spectacles, thinking only of Karl Appel as I attempted to read the number plate. 'No, Mr Bishop, the blue Ford Anglia, not the Hillman Imp.' It made no difference, I still got it wrong. But he took sympathy on me. Perhaps I got some of the numbers and letters right, because he let me carry on. It was a waste of time though. I didn't drive well and, despite all those lessons, I wasn't yet ready to drive. So it was back to Ernie for a few more lessons.

Ernie Entwistle was a jovial, bald-headed Lancastrian who lived in nearby Leavesden and had taught my mum to drive a few years previously. Dad said that any man who could teach my mother to drive a car was worth his weight in gold and should be heralded a hero. Ernie not only looked like my dad's hero, Fangio, he probably drove like him too. To be fair, as driving instructors go, he was great. He had a good sense of humour and a supply of sarcastic comments that he would reel out when you did something wrong, such as crashing into the kerb in the middle of your three-point turn in some leafy avenue in Abbots Langley, when Ernie would scream at you at the top of his voice, 'Don't do that, Curly!' accompanied by a hefty whack on the knee. Or yell, 'Slow down, Stirling!' into your left ear if you were going a tad too fast.

Ernie's tuition tactics might have been a bit on the eccentric side, but they worked, and a few months later I passed my test at the second attempt. Within a few days Dad had acquired an ancient Ford Escort for me. It had certainly seen better days and had been round the clock but, being my first car, I loved it dearly. Soon 'Ernie', as I christened it, started to look a little smarter. I gave him a good polish and acquired a few cheap extras like fake fur seat covers, one of those air freshener things that were designed to look like traffic lights, and a Watford FC sticker for the rear window. Dad reasoned – with uncanny accuracy, as it turned out – that the car would most likely be involved in a scrape or two in the not-too-distant future, so it was better not to splash the cash too much.

Laurie had become a member of the recently established Campaign For Real Ale (CAMRA) in the mid-1970s. The organisation had been founded a few years previously in the Farrier's Arms pub in St Albans. I soon accompanied him to this lovely old backstreet pub, and going out to St Albans and Bricket Wood pubs started to become a regular occurrence. I was born in St Albans and worked there for many years. If you liked good beer, it was the perfect place to drink it, having once had 90 pubs. Most of them get a mention in the following song, which appeared in the *Herts Advertiser* of 26th January, 1884.

THE CITY PUBS

I'll mention the name of each Pub in the Town,
North-Western, The Marlborough, The Anchor, The Crown,
The Maltster, The Post Boy, The Trumpet and then
White Hart, Two Brewers, and the famous Peahen.

Cross Keys, Potter's Arms, and the Queen's Hotel
The Duke, Bat and Ball, The Lamb, and The Bell;
The White Horse, The Wheat Sheaf, and Queen Adelaide,
The Cock, and The Peacock, and the naughty Mermaid.

The two Red Lions and the Fleur de Lis,
The Boot and New Inn, and the old Crab Tree;
The Wellington Inn, King's Head, and King Will.,
The Old Rising Sun, and the Little Windmill.

The Plough, The Harrow, The Stag, and the Hope,
The Bull, and Victoria, and the old Antelope;
The Vine, and Black Horse, Sugar Loaf, and Green Man,
The George, and George Tap, King's Arms, and The Swan.

The Farrier's Arms, the Verulam also,
The Rule and Compass, and the little black Crow,
The Lower Red Lion, Royal Oak, and the Queen,
The Cock and Flower Pot near the Woodman is seen.

Down to the Blue Anchor I have often gone,
And to The Black Lion, and Old Unicorn;
To The Rose and Crown, and little Six Bells,
Then back to The Painter to see Mrs. Wells.

The Blacksmith's Arms are close to his shop,
Then we go to The Sailor Boy, there must we stop;
We pass by the Cricketers on our way back,
And find The Beehive behind The Wool Pack.

There's old Garibaldi with a flaming red coat,
The savage White Lion and the tame little Goat;
The Hare and the Hound are in Sopwell Lane still,
And the two Fighting Cocks are down by the Silk Mill.

There's The Prince of Wales and Crystal Palace,
The young Farmer's Boy – the old Steeple Chase;
The Acorn, The Alma, The Eagle and Child,
And bold Robin Hood of the Forest so wild.

The Midland Inn and the Midland Hotel,
Three beershops kept by Blanks, Luck, and Bell;
The White Hart Tap is not in my list,
The old Golden Harp I nearly had missed;
Two in Pound Field whose signs I've forgot,
And the Pineapple is the last of the lot.

Laurie often consulted his new bible – CAMRA's *Good Beer Guide* – before we set out, and it would prove useful when we started to travel to Watford away games for the 1977/78

Third Division campaign. These were fun times to watch the team. Ross Jenkins and Luther Blissett had formed a great partnership in attack, aided by wingers Brian Pollard and Bobby Downes. 'Polly', a diminutive and tricky outside-right, was signed from York City in 1977, and Downes, a left-winger formerly with West Bromwich Albion, Peterborough United and Rochdale, was signed by Mike Keen in 1974. The defence included the ever-present John Stirk at right-back, with Keith Pritchett and Steve Harrison sharing the left-back spot. Ian Bolton, Alan 'The Fonz' Garner and, later in the season, Steve Sims were the centre-backs. Steve Sherwood and former Everton stopper Andy Rankin shared the goalkeeping duties. But it was the midfield duo of Dennis Booth and Roger 'Studs' Joslyn that made the team tick.

Appropriately enough, the first trip away was for the second leg of the League Cup clash with Brentford on 18 August. Laurie and I had no real worries during the 40-minute car trip down the M4, as two goals from Ross Jenkins and singles from Roger Joslyn and Bobby Downes had secured a commanding 4-0 lead in the first leg at Vicarage Road three days previously. As any beer lover knows, Brentford's Griffin Park ground is the perfect venue to watch football, as it has a pub on each corner of the ground. We settled for a pint of the local Fuller's London Pride in the Griffin before the game, which finished 3-1 to Watford thanks to goals from Ian Bolton, Alan Mayes and Bobby Downes.

The following Saturday was a scorching day. Instead of a trip to the beach, we opted for the delights of the West Midlands – Walsall, to be precise. Unbeknown to us, our hosts had a particularly nasty group of supporters back then, and a great many of them were drinking in one of the local pubs about half a mile from the ground. It was the very same pub that Laurie had picked from his latest copy of the *Good Beer Guide*, probably praising the quality of the Banks's bitter on offer there, but failing to mention it was also the fortress of about 100 neo-Nazis hell-bent on duffing up as many visiting football supporters as possible. Most of them were dressed in khaki military uniforms finished off with obligatory red and white football scarves. Luckily, the pub was at the bottom of a steep hill, so that by the time we got to within a few hundred yards of their watering hole, we could see a mass of green, red and white-clad lunatics running towards us. They didn't look like they wanted to consult us about the review the pub had received in the guide. It was then that Laurie twigged and said, 'Perhaps we'd better not have a drink here, Paul …' before turning round and rapidly legging it in the opposite direction. We had the last laugh though, watching Watford secure a 4-2 win. The natives were a resolute bunch, however, and keen to seek their horrible revenge by wreaking havoc after the match, marauding around any Watford fan or car they could find. Somehow we got away unscathed, but they were a particularly unsavoury bunch. They were so unsavoury that there was not a single member of the West Midlands police force to be seen.

The second-round League Cup game was significant and saw us come from behind to beat Second Division Newcastle United 2-1 at home, with two second-half goals from Luther Blissett. This was to prove to be a pivotal result as we were drawn away against Manchester United in the next round. That was something to look forward to. But in the meantime, next stop on our travels was a September trip to Gigg Lane for the game against Bury. Little more than 4,000 spectators gathered in the shabby stadium, and I reckon at least 1,000 were Watford fans. The only thing I can remember about the 2-1 win – apart from the goals from Ian Bolton and Ross Jenkins – was the amount of space the Watford fans had at the away end. We celebrated both goals by running around the terrace as if it was an athletics track. The gents' urinals were also interesting, consisting of an ancient wooden tray at crutch height that was extremely decrepit and covered with thick green mould and moss.

No matter, the following month it was off to Lancashire again, this time to the much posher Old Trafford for the midweek match against Manchester United in the third round of the League Cup. Laurie and I were joined by another person, making her one and only trip to a football match – our mum, Joyce. I have no idea how we managed to persuade her to make the trip north. She had never shown any interest in football before – or since, for that matter – not even batting an eyelid when England won the World Cup 12 years previously. But there she was, sat next to me in the fur-lined front passenger seat as we set off that Wednesday afternoon, 4 October. Looking back, I believe she simply wanted to spend some time with her two sons and sample something that we both obviously enjoyed doing. She wanted to share that pleasure with us. But whatever her reason, she was in for a treat.

We had good seats, level with the 18-yard line Watford defended in the first period. That first half was a disappointing one for Watford, memorable only for Joe Jordan's goal and some vicious racist abuse aimed at Luther. Graham Taylor tore into his team during the interval, accusing them of being frightened of United and to go out and impose themselves.

They took note and, within a minute, Luther soared above the United defence to meet a Bobby Downes cross and head an equaliser past Paddy Roche in the United goal. Laurie and I jumped up and celebrated while mum did a fair impression of Alf Ramsey, looking glum and remaining firmly in her seat. It was to get better 25 minutes later with a carbon-copy header from Luther, this time from Dennis Booth's deep cross. Laurie leapt up and down while I turned round, sank to my knees and started beating on my seat like Charlie Watts. I glanced across to my mother, who remained in her seat looking a little like the Queen Mother with the slightest hint of a smile on her face. We saw out the final 20 minutes or so to record a wonderful win. I've never been so excited at a football match before or since. Mum must have thought all games were like this.

A little over a month later, we travelled to the fourth-round midweek match at, of all places, Exeter. The trip west took us almost five hours, which included a pint and a bite somewhere near Dorchester. The game ended in a routine 2-0 win, with goals from Keith Pritchett and Ross Jenkins. By the end of the encounter, a mist to rival the one at nearby Grimpen Mire was beginning to appear, and by the time we were in Somerset it had developed into thick fog. We arrived home at 3am, shattered but happy with the win and the prospect of a quarter-final tie with Stoke.

One evening, a few days after the Exeter trip, Laurie suggested a visit to the nearby Fox pub would be a good idea. The pub was known locally as the Fox With Its Teeth Drawn, to distinguish it from the Fox and Hounds round the corner. It was situated about two miles out in the sticks, at the end of School Lane in Old Bricket Wood. When Dad heard we were going there, he reminded us to take care as the road's adverse camber meant that it was a notorious accident black spot. No matter, we were young, free and (fairly) sensible, and nothing scared us. It was a spring evening and still light when we started out on the short drive to the pub.

We settled down with our first pint, and a second soon followed as we played a few games of darts. It was approaching closing time when Laurie suggested another pint. We swiftly downed the final pint and left the pub for home. Halfway down the now dark and unlit road, I took a bend too fast and rolled the car. It flipped fully round, luckily, but as the road was narrow it was now wedged between two grass banks. We were both unscathed from the ordeal, which for me took place in slow motion. Once I got my wits back, I would attempt a very tight nine-point turn and drive home. But the problem for now was that the keys had disappeared, having flown out through the shattered windscreen. Laurie clambered out into the pitch black and returned almost immediately with the keys. If he hadn't, there would have been a strong possibility of an unsuspecting driver coming down the road and crashing into us. I turned the ignition and within a minute we were off home in a vehicle that was about two feet shorter than it should have been.

The roof had caved in so much that I was forced to drive in a style reminiscent of Marty Feldman's character, Igor, in *Young Frankenstein*. Very funny film, but there was not much to laugh at here. Dad came into our bedroom the next morning. Instead of the bollocking I was expecting, he was calm and philosophical. Rather than taking the 'I told you so, you never bloody listen' approach, he asked us if we were both OK and told us not to worry about the car as it was just a pile of metal. It was a write-off and, in Dad's mind, that was the end of it. I think he was more annoyed with my brother, feeling that he, being older, should have been more responsible. Anyway, I was soon allowed to drive Dad's company car, a bright-yellow Ford Cortina Estate, until I acquired a replacement. Dad's patriotism was apparent on the rear window where a large Union Jack flag was positioned.

Dad had recently started selling colour TVs produced in the UK by a work colleague, Derek Tyne, who owned Mill Hill TV. Dad and Derek often met for lunch, and Derek, who had secured a deal with Tesco, was a great character and raconteur. He told Dad that he had recently entertained some prospective Japanese clients in a plush West End restaurant. On another table sat Tesco owner Jack Cohen. Halfway through lunch Derek left his seat on the way to the loo and asked Jack if he could come over and say hello to him and thereby impress the Japanese contingent. Jack agreed. Five minutes later Cohen appeared as planned and cheerily greeted Derek, who replied: 'Fuck off, Jack, can't you see I'm busy?!'

The luxury of driving the Cortina didn't last long as Dad soon acquired a bright-red Datsun Cherry van for me. I have no idea why he chose it, but it came from a local garage, the owners of which my dad was fond of. He once said that a salesman is the easiest person to sell to. The car was good fun to drive, but a little noisy. On Saturday, 13 January, I was able to give it a good run as we had a 380-mile round trip to Swansea to kick off 1979. Swansea, along with Shrewsbury, were to be our main rivals for promotion that season, and already this match was being touted as a crunch game for both clubs.

We arrived in Swansea a little over an hour before kick-off and walked the mile or so to the ground. It was a bright day, but bitterly cold. After we'd been walking for a few minutes, a young lad of about 12 walked past us muttering to himself: 'It's off! It's off, I tell you!' and continued on his not-so-merry way. Laurie and I looked at each other in disbelief, hoping the boy had got it wrong. We quickened our pace and made straight for the ground. It soon became apparent that the game had indeed been cancelled, just moments earlier, when Swansea boss John Toshack had noticed a frozen patch of the pitch shaded by the main stand. Graham Taylor was furious and pleaded with the referee to play the game, for two reasons – in his opinion, it was such a small area that it wouldn't have been a problem for the players, and also to spare a thought for more than 1,000 Watford fans who had spent much time and money getting here. If it was going to be called off, the decision should have been made earlier in the morning. The referee was unmoved and the game had to wait until March to be played. We rather grumpily made our way back to the car to start the long journey back, although some friends later told me they went to the beach to enjoy a kickabout. At least they enjoyed a bit of football.

Luckily, we didn't have to wait long to watch the 'Orns in action again. It was just four days until we met the mighty Nottingham Forest in the League Cup semi-final first leg at the City Ground which, compared to Exeter and Swansea, was almost a home game! Forest were the top team in the country at that time, soon to become European champions at the end of that season, a feat they would go on to repeat the following year. This would be a real test. On the morning of the game, Dad took the Datsun up to the local shops to buy the morning newspaper. When he returned he expressed concern that the car's battery was a bit flat, suspecting a faulty alternator. The car was drivable but only for short distances. Attempting to get to Nottingham on a bleak midwinter Wednesday night was a waste of time. My brother and I knew better and decided to take a chance. It was the wrong choice. We broke down somewhere just north of Luton and had to call out the AA to be escorted back home, just in time to hear on the radio that we had been beaten 3-1.

Datsun duly fixed, we gave it a test drive to Vicarage Road to see the return game with Bury, which ended up an entertaining 3-3 draw. Then it was off to Oxford United on a snowy 27 January. It was an easy journey and we had time to stop off for a quick pint in Thame, before hitting a traffic jam on the main road into Oxford. It was there that Mr Capri Man had his moment. Although not Italian, he drove what was then the English equivalent of a continental car – a white Ford Capri – and we would often spot the car crammed full of his mates on away trips. He was over six feet tall and had the obligatory late-70s permed hairstyle, making him look a little like the curly one in *The Professionals.* By chance we were in the car behind when some local lads started throwing snowballs at anything resembling a Watford supporter's car. Mr Capri Man was an instant target and, after the second snowball hit the passenger door, he decided enough was enough, unwound himself from the driver's seat and slowly walked towards the louts. He looked a bit like Clint Eastwood in *The Good, the Bad and the Ugly* and he wasn't happy. He didn't have to utter a word before the lads legged it as fast as was possible in the slippery conditions. The game was the first time we saw Steve Sims play, and he put on an impressive display in the 1-1 draw. He even scored the Watford goal.

Three more away trips followed – Brentford, Mansfield and Shrewsbury. The Shrewsbury game was memorable for Ian Bolton's 'exploding wall' free kick that found the back of the net in a 1-1 draw. It was the first time the tactic was used and I'm not sure if it ever produced a goal again. The final home game of the season saw us crowned Division Three champions with a 4-0 drubbing of Hull City. Bolton and Joslyn were both on the scoresheet with, inevitably, Ross Jenkins and Luther Blissett scoring their 37th and 28th goals of a really enjoyable and exciting season.

CHAPTER 12
Six Players

THE SIX players featured here are my personal favourites from the time I started to support the club, from the mid to late 60s through to the early 80s. Four of them could be considered most fans' favourites, but the two midfield players were the type of footballers their respective managers – Ken Furphy and Graham Taylor – knew were vital. Terry Garbett and Dennis Booth were different types of player, but both personified what playing in the middle of the park is all about, mixing equal amounts of aggression, passion and creativity, and always trying to keep it simple. I have always had an admiration for this type of player, possibly because midfield was the one position I could never play in. I could tackle okay, but didn't have that almost manic desire and hunger to win the ball for the team. I also didn't have the energy to keep running from box to box. I remember a story that surfaced before England's World Cup triumph in 1966. Manager Alf Ramsey was with Alan Ball and Nobby Stiles in a park. Ramsey was watching a man repeatedly throwing a ball so that his pet dog could run and retrieve it. Ramsey said to Stiles: 'See that dog there, Nobby? That's what I want you to do.' Stiles replied: 'And when I've got the ball, what do you want me to do with it, boss?' Ramsey replied: 'Give it to Bobby Charlton.'

Six players. Just six. So where to start?

Ross Jenkins

One player epitomised the Watford spirit of the 70s and early 80s more than anyone else. When George Kirby signed Ross Jenkins from Crystal Palace in November 1972 for a then record fee of £30,000, 'money well spent' wasn't a phrase that was used by many fans on the terraces. At just 21, Jenkins wasn't the finished article, not by a long way, and he struggled to make his mark early on. Lacking confidence and standing 6ft 4in with a slim frame, he looked an awkward and frustrated figure back then. Two goals, both in the 5-1 win over Scunthorpe, from 21 games in his first season told its own story, and the following 1973/74 season was only marginally better – three goals from 18 appearances. In stark contrast, fellow striker Billy Jennings scored 25 goals.

To be fair to Ross, the team was on a downward spiral and underperforming under George Kirby, as Jenkins explains: 'There were a few personality clashes, which meant that some players didn't want other players doing well. That meant that team spirit was nowhere near as good as it could have been.' Despite new manager Mike Keen coming in for the 1973/74 season and improving morale, the club were relegated at the end of the following season. Slowly Ross started to improve and goalscoring became a bit easier, but it wasn't until Graham Taylor arrived in 1977 that his game came together.

All the players were transformed under Taylor's new regime, none more so than Jenkins.

After being appointed manager, Taylor immediately wanted to know everything about the players and quizzed Tom Walley about them. 'As mentioned previously, I told him there were some good players that hadn't been worked on yet, and who needed to learn the runs and work on the finishing,' Walley recounted. The brutal new training regime, married to Taylor's more direct way of playing, also benefited Jenkins. Taylor wanted to play with two wingers. In the early days it was Brian Pollard on the right and Bobby Downes on the left. Later Nigel Callaghan and John Barnes did the job. Luther Blissett, as Walley remarked, was also developing and would soon join Jenkins to spearhead the attack. 'We quickly slotted into this partnership because he was so quick and he matured very fast,' Jenkins explained. 'He was a strong lad and could run and bounce like nobody's business! He had a terrific shot on him and also was a great header of the ball.'

Jenkins played throughout the club's meteoric rise from the Fourth to the First Division. Ironically, he spent much of his time in the top division nursing an abdominal injury picked up in a game at Spurs, and this eventually ended his career. 'I came back and played in a big cup tie, against Nottingham Forest I think it was. That made my injury worse and I couldn't get myself to the fitness levels that my game needed.' He lists the famous comeback in the 1980 League Cup second-leg encounter with Southampton as his favourite game. 'I certainly remember it, especially as I was dropped for the first game. Graham called me over on the Friday lunchtime for a quick word. When you are asked for a quick word on Friday lunchtime, you know what is coming!

There was no problem though; me and Graham had a very good relationship. He would tell me he was resting me, and I would tell him he was wrong to, but that would be it, no fall-outs.'

Steve Sims

It was Saturday, 23 February 1980. Watford were entertaining Orient, although 'entertaining' might not be the correct word; it was a bruising contest. Early on, Orient centre-forward Joe Mayo was putting himself about a bit, making a few nasty challenges on one or two of our players. Sometime later there was a big skirmish in the Watford penalty area in front of the Rookery. I was standing on the Vicarage Road terrace and getting anxious as the ball pinged around in the six-yard box for what seemed like an eternity. The scene was similar to some footage of the Eton Wall Game I once saw on TV. It was a mess. Eventually the ball was cleared and all the players, bar two, trotted up the pitch to resume play. One was goalkeeper Eric Steele and the other, lying seemingly unconscious near the penalty spot, was Joe Mayo. We all immediately assumed it must have been Sims. Mayo continued to limp through the remainder of the game, which we sadly lost 3-0.

Prior to playing for Orient, Joe Mayo was with West Bromwich Albion. They were the team he supported as a boy and he arrived by an unusual route. His first club was Walsall, but he struggled to make the first team. Whilst playing for the reserves against West Brom, he scored a hat-trick. Manager Don Howe was impressed and signed him in 1973. He played more than 90 times for The Baggies before moving to Orient in a deal that saw a young Laurie Cunningham move in the opposite direction.

A few months after the Mayo incident, I was watching the team preparing to train at Cassiobury Park. Steve Sims was busy inspecting a couple of pairs of boots and asked – in a very mild, well-spoken voice – to nobody in particular: 'What footwear shall we wear today, chaps? Any ideas?' I was impressed and also pleasantly surprised as I was expecting a rougher, tougher northern accent to match Sims's rugged physique and features.

England under-21 international Sims was signed from Leicester City in December 1978 for a then record Third Division fee of £175,000. The previous most expensive Watford player had been Ross Jenkins at £30,000 six years earlier. As with most of the players and backroom staff who joined the club around this time, the reason Sims joined the club was Graham Taylor. Sims had known Taylor since he started to manage Lincoln City when Sims was a 15-year-old schoolboy playing for the local youth side and also training with Leicester City. 'Lincoln weren't interested in me until Graham went there, but my dad, who was an amateur centre-half with Lincoln, wanted me to get away from Lincoln and join Leicester.' This is exactly what Sims did, joining the First Division club in 1975 at 18. At the time, Leicester, under Jimmy Bloomfield, were known for their attractive football and, with players like Frank Worthington and Keith Weller, it was the place to be.

Unfortunately for Sims, in his first season at Watford he wasn't as fit as he should have been. Graham Taylor was aware of this early on, as Sims explains: 'When I first came in, it was amazing to me. Such a shock. At Leicester we never did any running. It was all ball work. On my second day at Watford we did a cross-country run in Cassiobury Park, up through the golf course, through the woods. Anyone who played for Watford when Graham was there will know this run. I was way behind. I had to keep an eye on the next one in the distance or I'd have got lost.'

Sims was made to feel at home quickly and he appreciated the helpful attitude of his new team-mates: 'The players were good for me. They were down to earth, normal people. I'd been brought up with Frank Worthington, who was flamboyant, to say the least, and the other "stars" and the way they behaved was starting to rub off on me. You don't realise it at the time but you start to change. They were the ones you looked up to. They were great players, but there were interesting things they got up to off the pitch and I thought "oh, that's normal is it?" I went to Watford and it was completely different. You weren't allowed to step out of line. After a while the dressing room evolved to look after itself in terms of discipline. First Sam Ellis, then Steve Harrison and then it was probably my turn to say to someone, "Hey, we don't do that here."'

Both Taylor and Bertie Mee were on Sims's side and were a real help. He did extra training with Bertie Mee to get fitter. 'He used to talk to me about defending too, when to tackle, when to wait. It was the people who made Watford: Tom Walley, Sam Ellis. People who worked hard and made you want to work hard too. I remember Sam from when he was at Lincoln. Graham wanted me to be more professional on and off the pitch, which is exactly what I needed, but at the time I didn't know it.' When the club had a bad spell during the 1978/79 promotion campaign, Sims was dropped. 'He did it for my own good. If we'd failed to go up it would have been seen as my fault.'

Sims was used to a more cultured style of football at Leicester and he liked to play constructively out from the back. How did he settle in playing a more direct game? 'He [Taylor] was direct, no two ways about it. He wanted to get the ball up to where you could score goals. It took a little bit of getting used to and there was a lot more to it than people thought. We worked morning and afternoon on the pattern, on the passes and making the runs. There was a lot more thought that went into it than people realised. And above all, it was successful. Over time it worked, as he got the right players in. It wasn't all success, success, success. The first year in the Second Division we were always looking over our shoulders and we were only safe with three games to go.'

Graham Taylor wanted Watford to play a more direct style of football, with the emphasis on fitness and high pressing. It was relatively easy during the rapid rise from Division Four to the Second, but once they were in the Second Division it got tougher. Taylor realised he needed new players who could fit in quickly with his style of football. 'He brought a few in for the short-term, to steady us in the Second Division and then replaced them as we went on,' Sims stated.

'Wilf Rostron came in as a winger and he was struggling to start with too. They were almost going to sell him, it just wasn't happening for him. I remember Graham took a few of us who'd been in the first team and we went up to Hereford for a reserve game. Steve Harrison, who had been left-back, was coming towards the end and Wilf played some of the game at left-back and I think that was the first time he saw something in Wilf as a defender. He was a hard little lad. He never bottled anything and when you see a bloke who's shorter than you getting stuck in like that it makes you raise your game.

'Malcolm Poskett came in up front, Martin Patching came from Wolves and he was brilliant, a really great midfield player, but he struggled with a bad knee injury. Pat Rice brought experience. You could see Graham bringing players in and weighing them up and working out who was going to help us go on. For 18 months it might have looked like the side was changing all the time but he was working it out in his mind as he went along.'

The club's youth policy then started to bear fruit, with Kenny Jackett, Steve Terry and Nigel Callaghan joining the first-team squad. 'That was probably no accident. It was the result of work with the youth players that Graham put in when he first joined the club. Kenny was magnificent. Really, really good. If he had been at a fashionable club he'd have been acknowledged as one of the best midfield players around. He was still just as good, but he didn't get the recognition. I think it was harder for us at Watford to get the credit we deserved.'

Things went well for Sims in that second season in Division Two, so well that he was named Player of the Season, but by the end of the 1981/82 promotion season he was struggling with his knee. 'I never really recovered from a cartilage operation I had when I was a youngster at Leicester. In those days they just took the cartilage out and left you with bone on bone. During the promotion season I got a kick on it and it swelled up and just didn't go down. I got fit and back in just towards the end and played the last month, including the Wrexham game where we clinched promotion. That was on the Tuesday night and on the Saturday we had Leicester at home. They were finishing about eighth. We won comfortably and after the game I bumped into a journalist from Leicester who always said to me, "Why did you want to go to Watford? You could have gone to a bigger club." I said, "This is why I went to Watford."'

John Barnes

John Barnes's first season was unforgettable. He was just about the best and most exciting footballer I had ever seen. In those early Second Division home games against the likes of Rotherham, Barnsley, Orient and Norwich, he tormented defences and captivated the crowd. When he received the ball out wide on the left flank, he was a revelation – direct, skilful, with every trick in the book and more besides. His crossing ability must have been a blessing for Ross Jenkins, Luther Blissett and Gerry Armstrong; hit with pace, often starting out between the six-yard line and penalty spot and curling away from the goalkeeper. He was quick, two-footed with perfect balance, and he could head the ball, so he really had everything.

John Charles Bryan Barnes was born and brought up in Kingston, Jamaica, the son of Colonel Ken Barnes and Frances Jeanne Hill, a journalist and TV and radio presenter. Barnes' father's job as commanding officer of the 1st Battalion Jamaica Regiment, and later Colonel, meant that John's childhood was disciplined but rich in sport. Ken was a keen sportsman, particularly fond of squash and football. He played football to a semi-professional standard, as well as captaining the Jamaican national side. Judging by his son's second name, he was also a big John Charles fan. Before moving to England with his family in 1976, Barnes had already met a young Bob Marley in Jamaica, and once in the UK he was used to being serenaded by Marvin Gaye, a friend of the family. Although John attended the rugby-playing St Marylebone Grammar School, he spent four years playing youth football for Stowe Boys Club in Paddington and later joined Sudbury Court.

The story of how John Barnes came to join Watford has several versions, but it seems a Watford-supporting taxi driver had seen him playing for Sudbury Court and recommended him to John Hardy, one of the club's scouts. Eventually Bertie Mee went and watched Barnes and, after ten minutes, saw that the 17-year-old was the finished article and got his phone number. When Ken Barnes picked up the phone and invited Mee to come over for an informal chat, he realised they had met several years earlier, when Arsenal played a friendly in Jamaica against the national team that Ken Barnes managed. They knew and trusted each other, which was important as John's dad was planning to return to Jamaica and wanted to leave his son in safe hands.

Tom Walley takes up the story: 'So he comes in for training on a Thursday night and we play him in a night game at Chesham. It was freezing cold. John Barnes's head was white and cold with the frost. Then he went to play a game away against Leyton Orient youth team. Graham Taylor came to watch it and he scored a free kick that went straight in the top corner. Graham Taylor said to me afterwards, "That will do me." And he signed him.' The fee was a new set of kit for Sudbury Court. It was the deal of all deals and within 18 months Barnes was playing for England.

Barnes, a modest, down-to-earth lad, tells a nice tale about a pair of Adidas 'Gerd Müller' football boots his dad bought him whilst attending the 1972 Olympic Games in

Munich. 'I loved those boots and was still squeezing into them two years later. I was a big fan of West Germany, especially after they won the World Cup in 1974, and I was the only one supporting them in the final against Holland.' During his early days in England, when asked which country he followed, he got a predictable response: 'They told me I'd better pick another team as they (the Germans) bombed our chippies!'

Barnes says Graham Taylor played a big part in his football career: 'He was a father figure not just to me but to all the lads. Nigel Callaghan could be a bit wayward and liked the odd night out so Graham would invite him round to his house some Friday evenings so he could keep an eye on him before the match. Cally wasn't a boy, he was 21 at the time!'

Graham Taylor knew his new signing 'was the last piece in the jigsaw' after Barnes put in a good performance on his debut at Chelsea in mid-September 1981. His fellow team-mates also knew his worth. Steve Sims: 'When John Barnes came to Watford there was a real buzz. The word went round that this 17-year-old was special. Quite a few of us went down to watch him play for the reserves when he first came. He was a lovely lad too. A total athlete. He was the best swimmer, the best tennis player, the best sprinter and the best cross-country runner.'

Before the season began, club captain and Arsenal double-winner Pat Rice played against Barnes in a first team versus reserves practice match. 'He gave me a hard time. His balance was terrific and he was so comfortable on the ball. He was clever too, rarely doing the same thing twice when he got the ball so you couldn't guess what he was going to do.'

His England career quickly took off and he found worldwide fame with a marvellous solo goal against Brazil in the Maracanã on 10 June 1984. The game was a friendly organised to commemorate the Brazilian FA's 75th anniversary, and Brazil had not lost in their home stadium for 27 years. Just before half-time, Barnes collected Mark Hateley's lofted pass on his chest, and from the left flank started to dribble 30 yards towards goal. First he beat Brazil's right-back, Leandro, followed by four more Brazilian backtracking defenders, before flooring goalkeeper Roberto Costa with a deft feint and slotting the ball past him. Barnes turned provider on 64 minutes, setting up Hateley to seal a 2-0 win. Barnes always maintains that if it had been a competitive game he would have been fouled before getting anywhere near the goal. Possibly, but Barnes scored many similar goals for Watford and Liverpool, and claims his first home goal for Watford against Rotherham was better. I saw that goal and 'Digger' was right!

Barnes achieved almost as much fame in 1990, only this time it wasn't on the pitch but on record. His rapping role on 'World in Motion', the official England song for that year's World Cup in Italy, helped the song top the charts. England's 1986 effort, 'We've Got The Whole World At Our Feet', had been so dire that when Barnes and the other players were told they needed to record a new song, most were not interested. However, 'World in Motion' was performed and produced by New Order and was, compared to previous efforts, in a different class. Nevertheless, only Barnes, Paul Gascoigne, Peter Beardsley, Steve McMahon and Des Walker turned up at the studio. Barnes got the rapping role and did a fine job on a great record.

Barnes was known as 'Digger' on the terraces, named after the Cliff 'Digger' Barnes character in the Saturday night soap *Dallas,* and when he left the club to join Liverpool in 1987, the Kop christened him 'Tarmac' because he was a black Heighway! Although his new nickname was a good example of Scouse humour, racism wasn't a laughing matter and was a big problem in English football during the 70s and 80s, but Barnes never let it bother him on the football pitch. 'I can't let ignorant people upset me. There were a couple of old Liverpool supporters who didn't want any black players in the team and as my first three games were all away, they'd never seen me. I scored on my home debut against Oxford United with a free kick and apparently one of the old guys said to the other, "He's not as black as I thought."' There was also the famous incident after an Everton supporter threw a banana at Barnes during a Merseyside derby. Barnes nonchalantly back-heeled it back where it came from, prompting the former Arsenal striker and now media pundit Ian Wright to comment: 'He was that good he could have peeled it with that left foot of his.'

Jamie Carragher says of Barnes: 'Technically the best player I've ever played or trained with, he was great with both feet and the best finisher I've ever played with. If you speak with the players from those great Liverpool sides and ask them who the best player they played with was, they all say John Barnes.'

Luther Blissett

When Luther Blissett broke into the first team in 1975, he was a raw but totally committed talent. He acquired the moniker of 'Luther Missit' from some national journalists.

Although his shooting could be wayward – sometimes nearer the Rookery *Watford Observer* clock than the goal – the crowd didn't take long to appreciate his direct running and powerful shooting. He was also pretty handy in the air. In time he formed an almost telepathic partnership with Ross Jenkins and they soon became the scourge of many defences …

Born in Falmouth, Jamaica, on 1 February 1958, Blissett lived just a mile from Montego Bay and remembers going there on the back of his dad's BSA motorbike to play his favourite sport on the beach. Luther, like many of his countrymen, loved cricket. But by the time he was five, the family moved to Willesden in north-west London and he soon started to play football at school. Luther settled in quickly: 'We had a great time as there was a large Irish population in the area and they, like us, loved music and they also loved to party.'

His junior football career started as a left-back, where he played until moving to centre-half aged ten. That could have been his permanent position but for a tactical switch made by his sports master late on in a game at Orange Hill. 'We were losing 1-0 with 15 minutes left when, in desperation, the teacher told me to play left-wing. I scored two goals and we won 3-2.' He joined Watford at 15 and signed as a professional in 1974 on £30 a week. 'I was about to start an apprenticeship as a motor mechanic when the chance to play football for a living arrived,' he said. 'I'd seen George Best and I wanted to be like him.' He got off to the perfect start, scoring on his debut in a 2-1 win over Swansea at Vicarage Road in April 1976, and he still remembers it well: 'Left foot, top corner.'

He also remembers running round the Vicarage Road pitch during a training session when Jim Bonser and Ron Rollitt appeared with a stranger dressed in a jacket with big lapels and even bigger glasses. Someone told him it was Elton John. 'I didn't have a clue who he was, I was into The Upsetters, Aswad and Bob Marley.' Luther loved scoring goals and it still upsets him that he failed to find the net in Watford's memorable 7-1 win over Southampton, *the* League Cup comeback of all time. And it also puzzles him that he didn't get the Player of the Season award in 1983 when his goals made him top scorer in Division One. Wilf Rostron got that accolade.

He might have been ignored by his peers, but Blissett's goals that season attracted the attention of AC Milan, who offered £1m for the top scorer in Europe. 'I received a phone call from Graham Taylor asking me to go to his home for a chat. That's when he told me the news.' Although he struggled in Italy, finding the slow-paced style of Italian football alien to him, he still enjoyed his season there. 'I'd recently got into the England team and Italy had just won the World Cup.' Blissett did suffer a great deal of racist abuse over there. 'I was used to it since school, unfortunately monkey chants and verbal abuse from fans and even players was common.'

Blissett, who is a host and guest speaker at Watford's home games, is a passionate promoter of racial equality and wants professional people to inspire all children, regardless of their skin colour, to aspire to obtain jobs in all sectors, including football clubs. 'I was a guest at the FA a number of years ago. I asked my hosts what they saw in the room? Apart from myself, there was not another black face, apart from those being put to work, serving. There are lots of jobs at football clubs where people of colour can and should be employed in those positions, just as they have people of white skin in those positions now.'

Terry Garbett

Thankfully there are still a few highlights available of those old Watford games from the late 60s and early 70s that show Terry Garbett at his best; in other words, a player who managed to move gracefully with the ball on a surface that often resembled a swamp, an ice rink or a muddy beach just after the tide has gone out. Poor old Les Simmons did his best, but either side of Christmas he was often fighting a losing battle. It didn't bother Terry though. In those classic cup games against Liverpool and Chelsea, you can see Garbett either looking for that killer pass or intent on running at the heart of the opposition's defence and having a crack at goal. A good example of this was his equalising goal in the FA Cup semi-final against Chelsea in 1970. Picking up a loose ball some 30 yards out, he glides across the yellow, heavily sanded ground before hitting a low shot from just outside the penalty area, which bounced prior to beating Peter Bonetti at his near post.

Yorkshire-born but Durham-bred, Terry Garbett began playing rugby at Blaydon Grammar School before his family moved to Chester-le-Street. It was there that he began playing football for the local school team, captained at that time by Howard Kendall, who would go on to join Preston North End and then Everton. After leaving school, Garbett played for several youth sides and one season scored close to 100 goals. Offers came from several clubs, but he chose to stay close to home and joined Middlesbrough for a short spell before Ken Furphy signed him for Watford in 1966. In all he played 200 games for Watford, scoring an impressive 46 goals. In 1976 he joined Furphy and his former Watford captain, Keith Eddy, at New York Cosmos, where he held his own among illustrious team-mates like Pelé and Franz Beckenbauer.

Dennis Booth

If there's one player who personifies Graham Taylor's view of the way football should be played, it is Dennis Booth. Although Sam Ellis and Ian Bolton were Taylor's first signings for Watford in July 1977, Booth joined the club three months later. Like Ellis, he played under Taylor at Lincoln. Although not known for his goalscoring during three successful seasons at the club, Booth started his football career as a 15-year-old striker for Charlton alongside team-mate Billy Bonds, who later became a long-serving legend at West Ham United. Booth left the Valley after seven years to join Blackpool, linking up with future Watford colleague Steve Harrison, before joining Southend for a two-year spell. He left to sign for Graham Taylor at Lincoln, missing out on promotion from the Fourth Division by goal average before going up as champions the following season. 'We had it wrapped up by April and scored over 100 goals and murdered that division,' Booth said.

The following year Taylor moved to Watford and Booth soon followed him, making 117 appearances in his three-year stay. 'Watford is a special club for me. We all knew something special was happening there back in the late 70s, even though some of us knew we would not be there to see it through. But I was there in front of the telly with my old Watford shirt and my cap on watching the Cup Final in 1984. The family loved it at Watford, it was very special. The players, the directors, the fans, the wives, we were all in it together. I lived locally and still have friends from those days. And there were those Bailey's nights! I have never known anything like that at any club. They were unique!'

When Booth mentions the fact that some players knew they wouldn't be there to see it through, he was one of them.

And the moment came when Kenny Jackett made his debut, replacing Booth in the 5-0 defeat at Sunderland in 1980. On the train journey home, Booth sat down next to Jackett and said: 'Well, that's it for me, son. It's up to you now. I'm an old man and I'll not play again.' He was right and left for Hull, where he stayed for five seasons before retiring.

And a manager – Graham Taylor

During that eventful, hugely enjoyable roller-coaster ride that was the 1978/79 season, Laurie sent Graham Taylor a letter just before Christmas, congratulating him and the team for playing such open and exciting football. My brother also added that he had not shaved, nor even trimmed his moustache, on superstitious grounds since early November, the start of an unbeaten run of league matches that lasted until mid-March. Within a few days Taylor had replied, thanking Laurie for his kind words and finishing with: 'May your moustache grow to handle-bar proportions!' Nice touch, and it shows how the manager knew the importance of PR and good communications. His father was a sports journalist and Taylor never underestimated the role the media – and the fans, for that matter – played in helping the club, his club, reach its goal. I didn't know Graham Taylor, had never met him, but for a chunk of my life he had been a big influence, a kind of football guru showing me the way. That he was ridiculed by the tabloid press, when things went wrong during his time in charge of England, was predictable but unjust all the same. He will be known to some as the man who said 'Do I not like that!' or 'Can we not knock it?' But I prefer 'You don't get cramp at this club!' and 'Easy goals at the back post.'

When he died in 2017, aged 72, the tributes came thick and fast. Outside his immediate family, I am sure nobody knew him better and longer (39 years) than the *Watford Observer*'s Oliver Phillips, who wrote: 'There were tributes to his dedication, his love of the game, which was his passion. The fact that he cared for his charges, his commitment to an extreme work-ethic and his undoubted honesty and sincerity were listed as qualities that earned him the reputation as a real gentleman of the game.' Phillips goes on to say: 'An unlikely source hit it on the head for me when Paul Merson stressed what Graham Taylor achieved at Watford will never be repeated or matched anywhere. "His was a blinding, outstanding achievement and anyone in Watford who doesn't appreciate that, knows nothing about football."'

One of Taylor's past captains was Pat Rice: 'I only had 18 months on the staff and I was still learning from him on the coaching side. You learn from great managers and he was forward-thinking and a great man, a hard wotsit but a true gentleman.' Another captain, this time Les Taylor, who led out the team at Wembley in 1984, admits that it wasn't until he left the club that he fully appreciated what he had done and shown him: 'He was way ahead of his time and was keen on the stats, but they were not possession stats, shots at goal had to be 20 or more per game.' Final word goes to Tony Coton: 'I owed him both professionally and personally in terms of the timing when he came for me at Birmingham. He got me away from that area and supported me. He brought me back to a club that I feel more warmly about every time I go back. What he did in court probably saved my life, let alone my career. A great coach, his man-management skills were terrific. I've worked with a few managers and for me he was on a par with Sir Alex. We had to be clean shaven, no jeans and we had to be courteous and not rowdy around hotels because he told us we were representing ourselves, the club and Graham Taylor. And I was proud to do so.'

And THE super-sub: Rodney Green

Testament to Harry Rodney Green's special place in Watford supporters' hearts came after his death in November 2018. In the obituary, in his home town of Halifax's local paper, they mentioned a special song joyously chanted by our supporters when the larger-than-life centre-forward scored a goal. It celebrated the goal and also his love of a drink or two in the local Vicarage Road pub.

During Watford's promotion push to the Second Division towards the end of the 1968/69 season, 'super-sub' Rodney Green became a folk hero, particularly for those in the Rookery. He made several cameo performances, coming on as substitute and scoring a few vital goals; the home game versus Bristol Rovers springs to mind when he scored the only goal. Cue that song: 'He's up, he's down, he's in the Rose and Crown, Rodney Green, Rodney Green!'

Seasoned journeyman Green also played for Halifax, Bradford Park Avenue, Bradford City, Gillingham, Grimsby, Charlton, Luton Town and Durban City in South Africa. Always with a smile on his face and a drink on his mind.

CHAPTER 13
Six Games

SIX GAMES, six cup ties. A surprise? Not to me. Watford players had learnt – from young, forward-thinking managers like Ken Furphy and Graham Taylor – that with the right game plan and attitude, the underdog from the lower division always had a chance against supposedly superior opponents. Here's proof that it's possible …

Watford v Liverpool, FA Cup sixth round, Saturday, 21 February 1970

I know that Liverpool hardman Tommy Smith was injured and that manager Bill Shankly started a rebuilding process to renew an ageing squad after this game, but I didn't know that then and I didn't care. No doubt Smith was missed. He was a frighteningly fierce and physical player, even for that era. Shankly famously said, 'Tommy Smith wasn't born, he was quarried.' Jack Charlton, a veteran of many Leeds versus Liverpool encounters, backs that up by saying Smith was the only player he was scared of. A few years after the game at

Vicarage Road, Smith scored Liverpool's second goal in the 1977 European Cup Final against Borussia Mönchengladbach to become an even bigger folk hero with the Kop.

When this particular cup tie was played, I was 14 years old and had been used to watching Watford take on the likes of Torquay, Tranmere and Lincoln. This was to be my February day of fun. I took up my new-found favourite position on the bend between the Rookery and Shrodells Stand and watched a first half that saw my favourite Watford player of the time, Terry Garbett, together with Ray Lugg, Stewart Scullion, Tom Walley and our answer to Tommy Smith, Duncan Welbourne, more than hold their own. Chief goalscorer Barry Endean had a couple of good early chances that just missed the target, and Lugg, skipping through the heavy mud, was starting to impose himself, skinning the Liverpool defence near the byline and sending in a superb cross. It was so good it fooled BBC commentator Barry Davies into thinking it was Scullion. Before the game, Watford manager Ken Furphy had highlighted a potential weakness with the Liverpool defence, and in particular centre-half Ron Yeats. Furphy reasoned that the bulky, 6ft-plus Yeats was great in the air but not so clever on the floor. And so it proved.

After a goalless first period, the second half saw Watford kicking towards the Rookery and I was in the perfect spot to witness the only goal of the game. Inevitably, man-of-the-match Lugg was heavily involved. Scullion earned a dubious throw following a challenge by Yeats. Lugg took it quickly and, after receiving the ball back from Scullion, nutmegged Phil Wall delightfully before drifting a perfect cross with the inside of his right foot towards the penalty spot. Endean read it perfectly and was on the move the moment Lugg crossed to head firmly past Tommy Lawrence. It was a great way to cap a great performance. The only mystery was that Lugg – whom Bill Shankly rated highly, having seen him score in a 2-0 win against Bristol City the week before the game – was only a bit-part player over a three-season spell at Watford. He was signed from Middlesbrough for £8,000 in November the previous year, but left the club for Plymouth Argyle in 1972 …

Watford v Chelsea, FA Cup semi-final, Saturday, 14 March 1970

Despite Brian Moore describing the pre-match atmosphere at White Hart Lane as 'wonderful', it didn't feel that way to me. I was standing with several thousand Watford fans in the lower terrace behind the goal. The upper tier was full of Chelsea fans who, when the mood suited them, showered us with sharpened coins. It was to prove a battle on the pitch too. Chelsea, third in the First Division table and managed by Dave Sexton, were red-hot favourites against a Watford side that was struggling near the bottom of the division below. Chelsea's team contained a mix of steel and silk – David Webb, Ron Harris, John Dempsey and Eddie McCreadie providing the steel, and Charlie Cooke, John Hollins and Alan Hudson the silk. But it was two of the former players, Dempsey and Webb, who combined to put Chelsea ahead after just three minutes. Dempsey met Alan Hudson's near-post corner and Webb bundled over from two yards out. Watford, who were without skipper and influential defender Keith Eddy, looked shell-shocked. However, on a heavily sanded pitch where flip-flops seemed more suitable than football boots, they responded immediately, with Stewart Scullion – soon displaying his distinctive hunchback-style dribbling – intent on taking on his fellow Scot, the international full-back Eddie McCreadie, at every opportunity. McCreadie was rattled and started to adopt an agricultural style of play that resembled a headless chicken. His attempts to scythe down Scullion at every opportunity added to the farmyard feel. Some minutes later, McCreadie's poor defensive header landed at Terry Garbett's feet. Garbett had one thing on his mind, advancing ten yards and unleashing a low shot from 25 yards that bounced before beating Peter Bonetti's outstretched right hand. Twelve minutes gone, all square.

Now it was the boys in blue who looked beatable, and they could – and should – have conceded again minutes later. Scullion was once again involved, receiving Duncan Welbourne's throw-in before beating McCreadie in the penalty area. This time McCreadie's scythe made contact and down went Scullion; a stonewall penalty. Schoolteacher and referee Gordon Hill thought otherwise. As if by magic, Dave Sexton moved McCreadie to the other flank, swapping him with David Webb. McCreadie's fellow henchman, Ron 'Chopper' Harris, then took out Terry Garbett as Watford started to dominate. Scullion and Garbett combined to put Brian Owen through on goal. Owen avoided another lunge from McCreadie, but his cross was cut out by Bonetti and the half ended a goal apiece.

Dave Sexton had said before the game that he admired Watford's team spirit, and he believed the fact that they had played together for so long was a big help. Ken Furphy's tactical nous was also a positive. Charlie Cooke, contained by Watford's Johnny Williams, and Peter Osgood, looked after by Walter Lees, were anonymous in the first period. But could Watford maintain their momentum and also get the bit of luck their play deserved? And could Terry Garbett continue to dominate in midfield? Both Cooke and Osgood, along with Peter Houseman, started to become more involved in an even first ten minutes of the second period. Alan Hudson and Ian Hutchinson then combined with Peter Houseman, whose left-wing cross found an unmarked Osgood to head home from six yards out. Gradually Hudson was starting to control things and, moments after Brian Garvey came on to replace Brian Owen, Peter Houseman's trickery and persistence resulted in him firing past Micky Walker with 17 minutes remaining. The tide on this beach-like pitch had turned and there was no way back for Watford. Another Houseman strike and one from Hutchinson gave Chelsea a flattering 5-1 win.

However, Watford did eventually make the news when they, along with Manchester United, became the first teams to take part in the FA Cup third-fourth place match. They were beaten by two Brian Kidd goals in a game played in front of 15,000 spectators at Arsenal's Highbury stadium on 10 April. Chelsea went on to beat Leeds United in the final, but they needed a replay at Old Trafford to do so after drawing 2-2 at Wembley. Mick Jones opened the scoring in that replay, but Peter Osgood equalised with 12 minutes remaining. An extra-time header by David Webb from an Ian Hutchinson long throw settled a two-part encounter that for the most part resembled a battle rather than a football match. Referee David Elleray reviewed the match in 1997 and concluded that the sides would have received six red cards and 20 yellow cards between them in the modern era. I wonder what he would have said about McCreadie's performance in the semi-final?

Manchester United v Watford, League Cup third round, Wednesday, 4 October 1978

When Graham Taylor arrived at Watford at the start of the 1977/78 season, he ushered Luther Blissett into his office to try and find out more about the young striker. Although Blissett had scored on his debut against Swansea City the previous April, he had failed to secure a regular place in the first team and the old regime were thinking of releasing him. Taylor wanted to find out why. He began to say his name to himself over and over again, each time emphasising it more theatrically, until finally, standing up and spreading his arms out wide, he cried out, 'Loootherrrr Bliiissiitttt' before sitting down. 'With a name like that, son, you're bound to be a star.' Luther wasn't sure what to make of it, but little more than a year later he rose to the occasion at Old Trafford.

Watford went in at half-time one down to a Joe Jordan goal, and didn't look like they would trouble United. Graham Taylor had other ideas and laid into his team during the break, accusing them of being frightened and imploring them to go out and make their presence felt. They did just that, and none more so than Luther. Despite receiving racist taunts throughout the match, it took him just seconds from the restart to make his mark, meeting Bobby Downes's cross with a soaring, power-charged header. Some 25 minutes later, an even better header from Dennis Booth's centre followed. It brought his goals tally to eight in as many games, including two in the previous round against Newcastle. Luther, an avid United fan, had truly arrived. In his first appearance at Old Trafford, he described it as 'a visit I'll never forget. The stick the crowd gave me never bothered me. People who resort to that are ignorant. The goals were all the more memorable because I don't get too many with my head.'

Chairman Elton John was just as happy: 'This was magic for me – the greatest moment I've known in football.' I would have to agree. But it wasn't a one-man show. Blissett was just starting to develop a fine understanding with fellow striker Ross Jenkins, while Dennis Booth and Roger Joslyn were tremendous in midfield, and Ian Bolton and Alan Garner solid in the centre of defence.

Watford v Southampton, League Cup second round, second leg, Tuesday, 2 September 1980

Another cup tie, another mountain to climb; and a steep one at that. Second Division Watford went into this second-leg encounter 4-0 down against First Division Southampton. Graham Taylor described that first-leg performance as 'inept and woeful' and that they had let themselves down. Before this game he told his team: 'Tonight I expect all Watford players to walk off the pitch and be able to look people in the eye.' The Saints were well established as a top-flight club and had recently bought England international Kevin Keegan from Hamburg. What's more, they went into this game unbeaten. Manager Lawrie McMenemy, later to become Graham Taylor's assistant when he was appointed England manager, rested a few of the regular players, including Keegan, which sent out a message that they thought the tie was over. Taylor got the squad together on the morning of the match and told them to treat it just like a league game, to try to get to 2-0 at half-time and then take it from there. Ross Jenkins sensed they had a chance before the game even started, noticing that Southampton were not mentally prepared. 'I thought if we could get off to a good start we might have a chance,' he said.

That's exactly what happened, with Malcolm Poskett getting on the scoresheet after just ten minutes, and the home team continued to play with pace and passion throughout the first period. Watford were creating a few chances, but it wasn't until ten minutes before the interval that Taylor and Watford got their second goal, courtesy of a left-footed strike from Ray Train. Despite Charlie George thumping a rasping drive against the bar early in the second half, Watford continued to press, with Ross Jenkins a constant menace to the Southampton defence. Eventually Martin Patching found the back of the net, but almost immediately Steve Sims deflected Graham Baker's shot past Eric Steele. With just over a quarter of an hour remaining, Watford still needed two goals to force extra time.

Within a couple of minutes, Ian Bolton converted a penalty. The crowd were going berserk by now, as was the new electronic scoreboard, with the dancing yellow men looking like they were about to blow a fuse! With seven minutes left, man-of-the-match Jenkins scored the vital fifth. Cue mayhem and extra time. Ray Train had clashed heads with an opponent and 17-year-old substitute Nigel Callaghan came on to replace him. As soon as he was on the pitch Watford won a corner and Callaghan positioned himself on the edge of the area. The corner was cleared straight to Callaghan who hit it first time into the back of the net. 'That was a special moment and I remember looking up to the Vicarage Road end to see a double-decker bus parked in the road and the people on the top deck must have seen the goal and were celebrating too.' Poskett added a seventh near the end to cap an unlikely and enthralling 7-1 victory. After beating Sheffield Wednesday at Hillsborough, Watford were rewarded with a fourth-round home match against European champions Nottingham Forest …

Watford v Nottingham Forest, League Cup fourth round, Tuesday, 28 October 1980

John Robertson was 5ft 8in tall, a little overweight, and looked and moved more like American TV detective Columbo than Cruyff. This Scottish outside-left wasn't quick and seemed to shuffle along rather than run. But he could destroy most defences in the world single-handedly, if the mood took him. He provided the cross for Trevor Francis to head the winning goal in the 1979 European Cup Final against Malmö in Munich, and then scored the only goal of the game that beat Hamburg in the final at the Santiago Bernabeu, Madrid the following year. Graham Taylor knew all of this and much more besides. He knew that if he could stop Robertson, he could stop Forest. And he had a plan. Taylor decided to man-mark Robertson with his experienced and disciplined centre-forward, John Ward. It was canny thinking on Taylor's part. Taylor was known as an attacking manager, but to come up with this defensive strategy and, more importantly, to choose the right person to carry it out was a masterstroke. Meanwhile Taylor's opposite number, Brian Clough, was so confident of victory that he left his assistant Peter Taylor in charge and was sunbathing in his holiday pad in Majorca rather than face a potential pre-Halloween nightmare in Hertfordshire. Forest looked good and full of composure and confidence early on, but two quick goals just before the interval – the first a penalty from Luther Blissett after Kenny Burns had brought down Malcolm Poskett, followed by a Ross Jenkins strike – did irreparable damage. Jenkins added two more in the second half to complete a memorable hat-trick. Ian Wallace scored a late consolation goal for Forest and John Robertson hardly got a kick.

Watford v Everton, FA Cup Final, Saturday, 19 May 1984

I was working for a local paper in the early 1980s and, instead of standing in the Holte End in the semi-final against Plymouth Argyle at Villa Park, I was sitting in the press box in the main stand. Of all the Victorian-era football grounds, Villa Park is my favourite, especially the enormous Holte End; intimate and intimidating in equal measure. I stood there with a work friend and Arsenal supporter, Rick Waghorn, for the FA Cup semi-final between Arsenal and Liverpool in 1980. As in 1984, the terrace was divided down the middle – Liverpool to the right and Arsenal to the left. The atmosphere was unbelievable. Both sets of supporters didn't stop chanting and cheering for a single moment. For the duration of the game I was singing all the Arsenal songs, because I had no choice. Emotionally, I couldn't help myself. The press box might have been good for my notes on the Plymouth game, but I knew where I'd rather have been.

In many ways it was a typically tense and tight semi-final, with Watford gaining a hard-fought 1-0 victory – George Reilly getting his head on John Barnes's near-post cross after 15 minutes. But Watford, used to being the underdog, struggled in the latter stages against their Third Division opponents. They just managed to hang on and their opponents in the final at Wembley would be Everton, 1-0 winners against

Southampton in their semi-final. Preparations for the final were not ideal, with Ian Bolton injured, Steve Sims struggling to recover from a broken ankle, and Wilf Rostron being suspended after being sent off against Luton at Kenilworth Road three weeks before the final. To make matters worse, young deputy centre-half Paul Franklin was recovering from a series of cartilage operations and would miss out. As a result, Watford would make history by fielding the youngest back four in FA Cup history – David Bardsley (19), Lee Sinnott (18), Steve Terry (21) and Neil Price (20). Taylor thought the younger players needed to know they were playing as early as possible, to settle their nerves, so he announced the team a week before. It was: Sherwood, Bardsley, Price, Taylor, Terry, Sinnott, Callaghan, Johnston, Reilly, Jackett and Barnes.

'I knew straight away I'd made a mistake but I didn't have the balls to alter the team,' Taylor later admitted. 'I thought the defence had handled Plymouth and the occasion so well, but as young players I felt they needed to know. The team had changed so quickly, we had this group of lads, so young, and they hadn't really gelled.'

Meanwhile Everton had played at Wembley only a few weeks before, when they lost 1-0 to arch-rivals Liverpool in the Milk Cup Final. They were a good team, but their manager Howard Kendall had been close to the sack and the two cup runs had probably saved his job. The Liverpool loss hurt the team, but Kevin Ratcliffe told them they had another chance and to stop moping. Once they'd reached the FA Cup Final, he told the players that they should remember how they felt after losing the Liverpool game, and that they didn't want to feel like that all summer. Watford had managed to train on the hallowed Wembley turf two days before the final, although nobody is sure how they wangled it. They even played a 40-minute first team versus reserves game.

After all the pomp, ceremony, pre-match hymns and protocol, the two captains – Les Taylor and Kevin Ratcliffe – shook hands beneath the beating sun and the game was underway. Watford started on the front foot, knowing how important the first goal would be. John Barnes's first-minute close-range header forced a routine save from Neville Southall. Soon after, two good chances fell to Les Taylor, who narrowly missed the target on each occasion. But it was Everton that got the first goal, seven minutes before half-time, when a scuffed shot from Trevor Steven landed at Glaswegian Graeme Sharp's feet and he turned to strike a low effort in off the post past Sherwood. After dominating for most of the opening period, it was a huge blow for Watford. It was to get worse with a hugely controversial Everton goal seven minutes into the second half. Trevor Steven put in a routine cross from the right, aimed for Everton striker Andy Gray. It seemed to be an easy take for Steve Sherwood who, at 6ft 4in, was more than five inches taller than Gray. However, Gray was a combative centre-forward and he came charging in for a header, more in hope than anything else. He managed to head Sherwood's arm and his momentum forced the ball to squirm from Shirley's grasp and roll into the unguarded goal. Some referees might have blown for the foul, but John Hunting unfortunately wasn't one of them. So, apart from a disallowed goal given for offside against Mo Johnston, Watford offered little else. Our day in the sun ended in tears. Kenny Jackett was my Watford man of the match, holding his own against England international Peter Reid in midfield.

One neutral spectator thoroughly enjoyed the final. England manager Bobby Robson, writing in the *Sunday Mirror*, said: 'It was a game for the fans. Overall Everton deserved to take the cup back to Merseyside. But Watford had their moments. They could have gone in at half-time 3-1 up instead of being a goal down. For me John Barnes lit up the match every time he was in possession. He loves Wembley and obviously he's going to be back there often.'

CHAPTER 14

Harry's Turn

FOOTBALL, BLOODY hell! Sir Alex got it spot on. Despite the deeply depressing fact that Watford have just been relegated from the Premier League, I am doing my best to placate my 11-year-old son, Harry, by explaining that the happiest days of my football life were spent supporting the club when they were in the bottom two tiers of the Football League. Harry didn't seem so sure about this, but he only took a day or two to understand my reasoning and is now looking forward to seeing Watford play the likes of Birmingham City, Sheffield Wednesday and dear old Swansea City, not to mention a trip to Brentford's new ground, no doubt minus the pubs on each corner. Sadly, barring a favourable cup draw, Craven Cottage will not be on the list. 'Poor old Fulham' joined Leeds United and West Bromwich Albion in the Premier League, replacing Watford, Norwich City and Bournemouth. Harry and I have been playing an amusing and entertaining game that involves predicting which of our so-called superstar players will remain to fight the arduous and brutal battle that is a season in the

Championship. 'Gerard Deulofeu definitely wants to stay, and Ismaïla Sarr will want to improve with us,' he chortles. I have no idea where he gets his information from, but I'd love to see Deulofeu's face when he steps out on to the pitch on a freezing-cold winter's day or night to receive a frosty reception from those friendly folk down the road at Luton. The Camp Nou it ain't.

Harry was born on 5 August 2009 and, with a bit of prompting on my part, took an early interest in football. At the ripe old age of five he started a few indoor taster sessions run by my old St Albans Wanderers mate, Darran Smith. Soon after this he signed up for some training at Roundwood Primary School in Harpenden. It was a step too far, too soon. The school has always had its own microclimate and, from October onwards, could be bitterly cold. Harry was happy for the first ten to 15 minutes, but once the cold set in he'd had enough. I reassured him that he could resume playing the game again when he wanted to, but in the meantime it might be a good idea to practise kicking with his weaker right foot. I didn't think about it again until about two years later, when he suggested we should have a kickabout in the local park. Within a few minutes I was surprised and pleased to see him using his right foot, and it soon became as good as his left. He's been two-footed ever since and, despite not being particularly quick, has that natural balance and ability to be able to go either way past a player.

By the age of seven he joined St Albans City Youth and is now in his fourth season with the Romans. Along with all of the other dads, I now get my football kicks by proxy, watching my son and his colleagues train and play week in, week out. To be able to play organised competitive football, receive regular coaching and training sessions – many of them on perfect artificial pitches and under floodlights – at such a young age, is marvellous and something to be cherished. They take it for granted, of course they do, and are playing for fun, experiencing the sheer joy of the game. They are Lionel Messi, just as I was Denis Law. Perhaps us dads take it a bit too seriously sometimes, but we are soon put in our place by our sons, who know better.

Shortly after he began that initial season, I took him to see his first game of professional football: Brentford versus Celta Vigo in a pre-season friendly at Griffin Park in July 2017. Since meeting my wife Begoña in 1997, I have adopted Celta Vigo, her local team in Galicia, north-west Spain. Despite Begoña hating football, she is now used to the two boys in the family either playing or watching the game. She and my eldest daughter, Elia, would much rather go shopping than waste their time watching a silly game of football. For a short spell I tried to entice her to accompany me to a few away games, but she was having none of it. I eventually tried to trick her into coming to an away game at West Bromwich Albion by asking her if she fancied a visit to the Hawthorns, believing she might think it was a retail outlet. I almost succeeded, but after thinking about it for a few seconds she replied: 'If it's a football ground, no!'

Back in the late 90s, Celta had a formidable team. They finished in sixth place in 1997/98, and under coach Víctor Fernández were fifth the following year and seventh in 1999/2000. Players included the Russian duo Aleksandr Mostovoi and Valeri Karpin, France's Richard Dutruel and Claude Makélélé, Brazil's 1994 World Cup-winner Mazinho, and Spain's Míchel Salgado. They never threatened the top of the table and there was a feeling they underachieved, but they played some superb football under Fernández. I once saw them produce a double-dummy manoeuvre that almost led to what would have been the perfect goal. That move summed up Celta – nearly but not quite. I've never seen it attempted since though. When Celta youngster José Ignacio Peleteiro Ramallo (Jota for short) joined Brentford in 2014, I followed his career in England. The game against Brentford was his last for the club before he joined Birmingham City and later Aston Villa. Jota scored one of Brentford's goals in a 2-1 win.

Harry's first Watford match followed some three months later.

Watford v Stoke City, Premier League, Saturday, 28 October 2017

Watford lined up thus: Heurelho Gomes (Brazil), Miguel Britos (Argentina), José Holebas (Greece), Christian Kabasele (Belgium), Kiko Femenia (Spain), Étienne Capoue (France), Tom Cleverley (England), Abdoulaye Doucouré (France), André Carrillo (Peru), Richarlison (Brazil), Troy Deeney (England). Subs: Andre Gray for Étienne Capoue; Will Hughes for André Carrillo. Manager Marco Silva.

The game was dreadful. Darren Fletcher scored the only goal of the game for Stoke early on, which was possibly the worst thing that could have happened, as they defended deep for most of the remaining 75 minutes and held on without much trouble. Watford were truly woeful. Indeed, Charlie Adam could have scored another from a rare breakaway, only to hit the post. I remember only two vaguely entertaining incidents from this wretched match. One was when Troy Deeney lost his temper with the diminutive Joe Allen and lifted him up by his neck near the end. This amused the Watford fans, but not Stoke manager Mark Hughes, who took offence at Deeney's behaviour. I can't recall the combative and aggressive Hughes showing too much charitable and sporting behaviour when he was a player, but no matter.

The other incident involved the Stoke supporters who were sat in the away enclosure near the corner flag at the Vicarage Road end. We were sat at the far end of the Elton John stand, in other words right next to the rather boisterous Stoke fans who spent most of the match singing their heads off. They were winning away and having a good time. I did notice Harry looking at me in a confused and quizzical way when some of the language became a tad fruity. Eventually he asked me what they were saying and I truthfully replied: 'I have no idea.'

Since the Stoke game, Harry has taken in home games against Liverpool, Southampton, Everton and Burnley, and in a short space of time has witnessed some of the highs and lows football supporters enjoy and endure in equal measure. The goals, gasps of the crowd, the songs, the swearing, near misses and bad decisions. The reading of the programme, drinking of Bovril, beer or fizzy drinks. And the discussions and debates in the car on the way home, munching a portion of chips whilst listening to the results and reports on the radio.

Liverpool's visit on Saturday, 24 November 2018 was viewed from pitch-side seats in the Graham Taylor stand, where we had a perfect view of Will Hughes being fouled in the 67th minute whilst attacking the Liverpool goal and referee Jon Moss waving play on. The game was goalless and, from then on, Harry was to see a perfect example of Murphy's football law, which reads: when you miss a good chance or get a wrong decision, the opposing team will immediately go down the other end and score. And so it came to pass. Liverpool countered and within seconds Mo Salah put Liverpool one up. Further goals from Trent Alexander-Arnold and Roberto Firmino gave the visitors a 3-0 win. The only consolation we had was to watch Jordan Henderson unravel before our very eyes when he disputed a throw-in decision not five yards away from where we were sitting. The game was in its final few minutes, done and dusted, but Henderson had lost it and for some unknown reason was apoplectic. The red mist was swiftly followed by a red card.

The next game was to introduce Harry to the vagaries of schadenfreude in football. As most football followers know, Watford have had their fair share of managers over the past few years. We have almost got used to it without fully understanding the reasons as to why the powers that be feel the need to change a coach every few months or so. But it's not always our fault, honestly! Take Marco Silva. Everton did, and they got into a lot of trouble for poaching our Portuguese boss three months into the 2017/18 season. From November to January, the form and focus disappeared alarmingly, to the extent that we gained a paltry five points from ten Premier League games. Silva was sacked on 28 January, with the club claiming 'the unwarranted approach by a Premier League rival' had caused 'significant deterioration in both focus and results to the point where the long-term future of Watford FC has been jeopardised'. We subsequently received £4million compensation and a new manager. Javi Gracia. However, there were still problems. Our star player, the promising and exciting young Brazilian winger Richarlison, had more or less downed tools after Silva left. Silva had become something of a father figure to the Brazilian; a shared language possibly played a part in this. So with Richarlison pining for Silva, it was no surprise he was sold to Everton on 24 July 2018 for a fee that allegedly started at £35 million and rose to £50 million. I hope you're keeping up with all this because it's worth it, I promise you.

To say Watford fans were looking forward to Silva and Everton's return to Watford on Saturday, 9 February 2019 is a slight understatement. OK, we had to wait 377 days and 65 minutes, but it was time well spent. After a dull first half, our manager Javi Gracia must have given the players a pep talk at the interval, as the tempo quickened in the second period. Kurt Zouma almost put through his own goal following a José Holebas corner after 55 minutes. Then ten minutes later Watford scored, Andre Gray tapping in Will Hughes's cross from close range. Cue instant pandemonium. For the rest of the game Harry and myself joined the rest of the Watford crowd singing a song to Marco Silva: 'He's better than you, he's better than you, Javi Gracia is better than you.' Richarlison was anonymous throughout and was substituted late on. Oh, and Zouma still had time to get sent off. Revenge never tasted sweeter.

The Southampton game on 23 April 2019 featured the quickest goal in Premier League history, when Shane Long scored after 7.69 seconds. This terrifying fact is made even harder to comprehend when you consider it was Watford's kick-off. The ball was played back to centre-half Craig Cathcart, whose attempted pump up the pitch was charged down by Long who calmly lofted the ball past a bemused Ben Foster. Andre Gray rescued a point when he equalised in the last minute.

All the excitement surrounding the Everton win and the early and late goals in the Southampton game were just a memory when we welcomed home an old friend, player and manager, Sean Dyche, on 23 November 2019. Naturally we had acquired a new manager by this time, Quique Sánchez Flores having commenced his second spell at the club ten weeks previously, after Javier Gracia was sacked.

Sean Dyche began his football career in 1989 as a centre-half for Nottingham Forest's youth team while Brian Clough was manager. He left after little more than a year to join Chesterfield, where he became captain. Spells at Bristol City, Luton Town (loan) and Millwall preceded a three-year stint at Watford that commenced in 2002 … He finished his playing career at Northampton Town before returning to Watford as under-18s coach in 2007. Two years later he was promoted to assistant to the newly appointed manager Malky Mackay. When Mackay left to manage Cardiff City in June 2011, Dyche became manager, helping the club to finish mid-table in the Championship before being replaced by Gianfranco Zola at the end of the season.

Dyche then started his hugely successful period with Burnley, replacing Eddie Howe as manager in October 2012. He's been there ever since, moulding them into an established Premier League team after two promotions from the Championship. With his sergeant major manner, coupled with a throaty growl, Dyche has Burnley playing in a typically combative way. Hard work is the key, something Graham Taylor would have been proud of. Dyche is also similar to Taylor in the way he values the importance of team spirit, often referring to his players as 'the group'. He also likes Burnley to play in a direct and physical way. They are always difficult to play against and dangerous at set pieces. Burnley, under Dyche, consistently punch above their weight.

Quique Sánchez Flores and Sean Dyche are poles apart. While Dyche barks, Sánchez Flores whispers. Whilst he might not be well known in England, the opposite is true in Spain. The son of actress Carmen Flores and nephew of flamenco singer and dancer Lola Flores, Quique's godfather was Alfredo Di Stéfano, and his father, Isidro Sánchez García-Figueras, played with Di Stéfano for Real Madrid in the mid-1960s. Quique also played right-back for Los Blancos for two seasons, but is best known for a ten-year stint with Valencia starting in 1984.

Harry and I enjoyed a bit of a VIP day for the home game against Burnley, being accompanied by Javi Gracia's analyst, Isidre Ramon Madir, and his son, Marc. We sat in the players' enclosure and were greeted by many of the Watford backroom staff eager to welcome Isidre back to the club. We met Isidre and Marc when the latter joined Harry's team in St Albans at the start of the season. Previously, Isidre had spent nine years working as an analyst for Luis Enrique at his local club, FC Barcelona, before moving on to work with Gracia. Watford, who started the game in 18th place, were the better side during the first period, with Gerard Deulofeu a constant threat. He twice forced Burnley goalkeeper Nick Pope into making fine saves, but the sides went in at half-time level.

More worrying than the home side's lack of a cutting edge in front of goal was an injury to Craig Dawson, which prevented him from reappearing for the second half. Isidre looked worried and told me Dawson was vital as he organised the defence, particularly at set pieces. And so it proved. Within eight minutes Chris Wood had hooked the ball past

Ben Foster following a corner. Watford were still playing well in patches and causing problems for Burnley's defence, but still didn't look likely to beat Pope. Ashley Barnes' late penalty after a José Holebas foul and a James Tarkowsski goal two minutes from time gave Burnley a 3-0 win. Watford ended the day bottom of the table, but Harry didn't mind as James Tarkowski gave him a wave and a smile as the Clarets ran off the pitch. Maybe Tarkowski knew something we didn't and was waving goodbye to Watford and their five-year stay in the Premier League.

So Harry and I will be watching Watford play in the second tier of English football. With the uncertainty surrounding the coronavirus pandemic, we may well have to watch the games on TV rather than live. But, along with all football fans, we will enjoy this enforced modern alternative, because any kind of football is better than no football at all. Or as Danny Baker put it, in replying to a reporter who thought there was too much football on TV: 'No, there's not enough.'

BS